Contents

Activities   137

A Guide to Teaching Information Literacy:
101 Practical Tips

Helen Blanchett, Chris Powis and Jo Webb

LEARNING
RESOURCES
CENTRE

facet publishing

© Helen Blanchett, Chris Powis, Jo Webb 2012
Published by Facet Publishing
7 Ridgmount Street, London WC1E 7AE
www.facetpublishing.co.uk

Facet Publishing is wholly owned by CILIP: the Chartered Institute of Library
and Information Professionals.

British Library Cataloguing in Publication Data
A catalogue record for this book is available from the British Library.

ISBN 978-1-85604-659-6

First published 2012
Reprinted digitally thereafter

Mixed Sources
Product group from well-managed
forests and other controlled sources
www.fsc.org Cert no. SA-COC-1565
© 1996 Forest Stewardship Council

FSC

Text printed on FSC accredited material.

Typeset from author's files in 10/14 pt Palatino Linotype and Frutiger by Facet
Publishing.
Printed and made in Great Britain by MPG Books Group, UK.

Introduction

About this book

Why yet another book on information literacy? The answer is quite straightforward: because we wanted to provide a different kind of resource, that we hope will be of practical benefit to practitioners developing learning, teaching and training in the library and information world.

There is a huge amount about information literacy published every year, ranging from theoretical overviews of the nature of information literacy to case studies of the applications of different pedagogical approaches. Articles, book chapters and books cover a variety of critical, discursive, reflective, research-focused, qualitative and quantitative approaches.

We wanted to do something a little different. Rather than prepare lots of case studies of how it went well (there are plenty of other places to get that kind of information), we decided to compile a series of hints and tips, together with some best practice guidelines. Using this book should help to extend your teaching repertoire, suggesting novel approaches to some regular teaching conundrums and be a useful resource for definitions and background information.

Most of the tips are especially relevant for those of you running a structured teaching or training event. This might be in formal education (in schools, colleges and universities), in public and community settings, in health services or in corporate settings. Increasingly this kind of work – essentially moving beyond doing presentations to leading interactive learning events – is key for nearly all of us.

As experienced practitioners, we hope that the book will provide practical advice, underpinned by our experience and theory. We have deliberately tried not to make this too academic a text, as we think there are other, more useful works to support the development of your knowledge and understanding in this area. So, although we do include references to useful additional sources these are by no means intended to be exhaustive. We do want this book to help build your confidence as a teacher. It should provide you with a starting point for experimenting with different teaching methods and strategies.

But remember, you need to develop your own ideas and teaching styles and we hope that this book will provide a source of guidance and inspiration as your experience grows.

Using this book

The title of this book is a misnomer. Although it is organized into a series of 101 tips, each tip in itself has a variety of options and advice. Although we are not suggesting that this is a multidimensional text, do note that if you follow each of the variations within a tip you will find yourself with many more practical hints and advice than the number advertised in the title.

The tips are divided into three sections:

- Planning – provides a grounding in planning, design and theory
- Delivering – practical guidance for you as a teacher, trainer or presenter in developing your own skills
- Activities – a range of specific activities to use in teaching.

Although this book has not been written with the intention of being read in a linear fashion – it is designed to be dipped into as and when required – 'Planning' can be read sequentially in order to provide a good grounding for planning teaching.

Each tip has an overview and details of the tip or activity, guidance on when to use the tips and some issues to watch out for when trying out the techniques. One of the most important parts of each tip is the *More* section, where we give further ideas and suggestions to adapt and extend the tip. We hope these ideas will prompt you to think about ways you can adapt the tips to your own teaching situation – it is important to experiment!

We hope you find this book an invaluable support to your teaching activities.

Note: the book often refers to Virtual Learning Environments (VLEs), which are known elsewhere as Learning Management Systems or online learning environments.

Acknowledgements

We would like to thank colleagues at De Montfort and Northampton Universities, JISC Netskills and elsewhere who have shared their ideas about teaching over the years.

Special thanks to Nigel Morgan and Linda Davies at Cardiff University for letting us discuss the Cephalonian method again; Kaye Towlson for sharing the Information Source Evaluation Matrix; Steve Bond at LSE for his advice on audio feedback; Katrina Little at Kilmacolm Nursery for her fantastic Blooming Blooms activity; Jude Carroll for the 'Drawing the Line' plagiarism exercise; Connie Malamed for her storyboard template; Sara Bird at Newcastle University for her mind map and Jane Clarke for her feedback on an early draft of the book.

In addition many thanks to colleagues at JISC Netskills: Dave Hartland for his wise words over the years and permissions to include JISC Netskills materials, Danny McAtominey for making practical sense of learning and teaching theory, Chris Thomson for guidance on digital storytelling and Steve Boneham for advice on social media and podcasting.

We would also thank our families, in particular Dylan and Elinor who have brought much joy and a little delay to our writing.

Planning

1 A framework for designing and delivering teaching and learning

Learning and teaching events must be based on an understanding of how to create effective learning opportunities. This does not mean that every session you plan needs to be influenced by extensive reading of the pedagogical research for each type of activity, but rather that it is vital that you establish a baseline understanding of core teaching theory and how it relates to information literacy and the library and information context.

There are disputed philosophies of teaching, based on quite different conceptions of the world, for example:

- Sociological theories of teaching rest on the idea of groups, communities and societies.
- Psychological theories often emphasize cognitive development, involving information processing and development of thoughts and ideas
- Behaviourist theories focus on the idea of conditioned learned behaviour often dominated by the teacher.
- Constructivist theories involve the learner making connections for themselves and being encouraged to link to prior knowledge and experience.

Do note that when we write about a 'teacher', we mean the person leading or designing a learning and teaching opportunity – you. When we write about 'sessions', we mean a learning and teaching event in any form, including interactive learning online or self-guided learning materials. Vocabulary is difficult in this sphere.

From a practical perspective, the most useful approach your authors have used in designing, delivering and reviewing teaching is the framework drawn up by Geoffrey Squires (1994). This can be applied very effectively to the library and information context. It has three parts:

- the optimal conditions of learning
- the functions of a teacher
- variables in teaching.

Squires (1994, 17) discusses the optimal conditions of learning, which are grouped under four headings – person, process, information, environment:

- The person who learns must have a *positive self-concept*, an *open mind* and the necessary *ability* and will *prioritize* the learning activity.
- The process must be *active* (learning by doing), *reflective* (so information can be internalized), with suitable tasks that enable the *processing* of *information*.
- The information that is learned should be *patterned, meaningful, embedded* (part of a curriculum or which can be integrated into work or life) and *embodied* (usually in the teacher, but perhaps in peers or family members).
- The environment in which learning takes place should offer *stimulus, support, feedback* and *reward*.

Other tips in this book discuss the learning situation in more detail, but this summary should be very helpful in auditing your own teaching situation and especially in identifying areas that need to be given priority in planning.

Learning often needs facilitators or teachers to guide the learners and to structure learning opportunities. Squires (1994, 38) lists the functions of a teacher being to:

- motivate
- audit
- orientate
- inform
- explain
- explore
- develop
- exercise
- appraise (or assess)
- reinforce.

There are tips throughout this book for each of these functions.

We should emphasize that although there may be some distinctive aspects to teaching as a library and information professional, the core principles of teaching remain the same. What you will find are many different variables, including:

- Rationale: what is the purpose of this session?
- Context: why is this session taking place?

- Process: what kind of teaching methods will you use? How will the session be structured?
- Level: what age and skill level are you working with?
- Group: what are the group dynamics? Is it a large or a small group?
- Individual: especially if working with smaller groups, the impact of individual learners is very noticeable.
- Self: how do you feel? We do not all teach the same way (nor should we) and we can have good days or bad days; we can like or dislike our material, or sometimes be less confident than usual.
- Physical setting: is the room suitable and set out the way that you need it to be?
- Organizational setting: is the wider organization supportive or not? Is this session seen as a good thing or not?
- Social setting: do your learners know each other? Is it a social gathering? Are there cultural or group issues?

Each element of the framework contributes to effective teaching.

Identifying which aspects of the optimal conditions of learning may be most challenging (and which the most straightforward) will be a starting point in planning your learning and teaching event. If you know your learners may not prioritize the learning, think about how you can link it into assessments or their core activities; if your physical environment is less than ideal, think about how you can compensate for its limitations.

The second element, which covers the functions of a teacher, should be the basis for designing your learning and teaching event – think about how you will perform each of these functions.

Finally, the variables means that you should not rely on 'recipes' for success: variables influence the outcomes of any teaching that is undertaken and you need to be flexible and responsive to contingencies.

✓ BEST FOR

- This framework can be applied in all learning and teaching contexts for any discipline or level.

✚ MORE

- The variables are always going to change – it is their nature.

Consideration of the variables will influence the shape and nature of whatever learning and teaching event you plan.

! WATCH OUT

Be careful of:

- Orthodoxy: This is perhaps a rather extreme term for always taking the safest, least ambitious path in planning your teaching. Sometimes you should take risks and try out a completely different plan for your session. It can be tempting to believe that there is a 'right way' of teaching a specific topic, but this is not true: there are many effective ways of teaching the same content.
- Imbalance: Sometimes you can focus too much on one part or issue of your teaching without stepping back and thinking about the whole learning experience. This is manifested in many different ways: you might spend too long on one part of a topic (e.g. password management) and lose the interest of your learners; or you might be so keen on a particular teaching approach that you incorporate it into sessions which may not be suited to it.
- Theory: Effective teaching is a balance between applying your knowledge of pedagogy and sensitivity to immediate circumstances. Finding out more about learning and teaching, reflecting on your practice and evaluating what you do are essential parts of teaching. But be careful you do not let external rubrics dominate teaching situations.

↔ REFERENCE

Squires, G. (1994) *A New Model of Teaching and Training*, University of Hull.

→ FURTHER READING

Atherton J. S. (2011) *Learning and Teaching*, www.learningandteaching.info/learning. (A UK academic's overview of learning and teaching theory, a good place to start for an overview.)

2 Information literacy and standards

There are many information literacy (IL) related standards and definitions globally. The UK's Chartered Institute of Library and Information Professionals (CILIP) defines information literacy as 'knowing when and why you need information, where to find it, and how to evaluate, use and communicate it in an ethical manner' (www.cilip.org.uk/get-involved/advocacy/information-literacy/pages/definition.aspx).

Following on from that definition, in order to be information literate an understanding of the following skills or competences is required:

- a need for information
- the resources available
- how to find information
- the need to evaluate results
- how to work with or exploit results
- ethics and responsibility of use
- how to communicate or share your findings
- how to manage your findings.

There are several frameworks, although the US ACRL (Association of College and Research Libraries) and UK SCONUL (Society of College, National and University Libraries) models (see references) are two of the most often applied. In the teaching context, these frameworks can serve several purposes:

- To let others know what information literacy is all about, by providing a statement of what IL is, and making explicit the range of competences and knowledge encompassed by IL.
- To act as a reminder of the range of skills you should be supporting.
- To act as a benchmark (although levels are often not built in) to assess against.
- To be something that can be mapped against the curriculum.

- To map to organizational strategy, and thus emphasize the value of information literacy.

At national level, information literacy standards are useful in policy development – for example, the national information literacy projects in Scotland (www.gcu.ac.uk/ils/framework.html) and Wales (http://library.wales.org/en/information-literacy/national-information-literacy-framework) – and sometimes within organizations.

IL frameworks and standards have their limitations in that they often do not mean anything to learners – IL needs to be contextualized for the learners. These are skills that are used for a purpose, so mapping these standards to curriculum or other outcomes shows the relevance.

Consider how you will use the frameworks and language carefully – it may be that these are more appropriate to guide your own planning and development, but need to be translated into the language of your learners and collaborators. It may be that your learners never need to see the IL framework itself! If you are lucky enough to work in a context where information literacy is an accepted term and perhaps even a requirement within courses, then presenting the frameworks and related language should not be a problem.

✓ BEST FOR

- benchmarking a curriculum
- policy development
- auditing practice.

✚ MORE

- Look at IL frameworks and compare elements. Think about how they apply to different levels of learning – sometimes IL frameworks do not differentiate between simple and complex information needs effectively. See **Facilitating learning** for guidance on levels of learning and how this relates to the needs of your learners.
- Use the standards to link to the curriculum and map against this where you can. This will enable you to demonstrate and promote the relevance of IL to both staff and learners. However, this can be a time-consuming and laborious task, so it's worth checking to see if anyone else in your sector has already done this!

- Consider mapping to other frameworks that may be relevant, for example graduate or professional attribute frameworks. Look for any opportunity to demonstrate the relevance of information literacy to specific occupational knowledge requirements.
- Consider mapping the learning resources available to frameworks – however, bear in mind that learners may not be familiar with the model or framework.
- Most information literacy interventions involve the early stages of the models (i.e. planning and finding). Try to think creatively how you can support other stages – this may involve working closely with teachers or lecturers to explore curriculum requirements.

❗ WATCH OUT

- Many models encourage a linear view of the development of information literacy. While this can be appropriate (e.g. the Big6 (www.big6.com/about) is designed to teach approaches to problem solving and research), it can lead to an over-simplification of IL behaviour. This 'linear' approach does not conform to what is known about information behaviour, which is rarely linear.
- Nor are the models always especially sensitive to different levels or types of information need and the patterns of knowledge and publishing in different disciplines. Ensure that your interpretation of the IL models and frameworks is matched to your learner's context. In the UK, SCONUL 7 Pillars model is being revised to address this, by presenting the model in a less linear way and beginning to create contextualized 'lenses' on the model, for example its 'researcher' lens.
- Applying the standards can be problematic if they are used in a tick box approach that ignores the complexities of information behaviour. With IL this can lead to a mechanistic task focus rather than the complex cognitive processes that underpin real understanding. A simple example would be when teaching the mechanics of citation without exploring why we use references when we write.
- Consider whether it is viable and reasonable to cover all parts of your selected information literacy standards within your learning and teaching event. For example, if your session is part of a programme of learning, check that you understand how it fits into the course as a whole. Library and information professionals are not the only people responsible for

learners developing information research, handling and evaluation, so, for example, evaluation or citation may be integrated into another part of a course and taught by different people.

• Be careful about using the term 'literacy' as implying someone is 'illiterate' can sometimes offend.

❖ REFERENCES

Association of College and Research Libraries (ACRL) (2011) *Information Literacy Competence Standards for Higher Education*, www.ftrf.org/ala/mgrps/divs/acrl/standards/informationliteracycompetency.cfm#stan.

Society of College, National and University Libraries (SCONUL) (2007) *Seven Pillars of Information Literacy, Core Model for Higher Education* and the *Research Lens for Higher Education*, www.sconul.ac.uk/groups/information_literacy/seven_pillars.html.

3 Training Needs Analysis (TNA)

A Training Needs Analysis (TNA) is a formal process of identifying a training gap and its related training need. It can be utilized before designing your information skills teaching or as part of a session. In the former case it should be done in partnership with the other key players – learners and those who might arrange or book the teaching (see **Pre-session audit** and **Collaboration** for further tips).

TNA is primarily used in business contexts to match individual training needs to organizational priorities and goals. More typically in the information literacy context, you will prepare a TNA as part of a programme plan or as a bid for time or resources. The TNA will need to be informed by wider plans – a teaching and learning strategy in a formal educational setting, perhaps. A TNA can help you pitch a proposal for the teaching of information literacy as a catalyst for organizational and/or personal change by linking current knowledge and skills with future requirements.

Starting points for a TNA will be an analysis of current and future requirements in terms of knowledge, skills, attitudes and competences. In a workplace setting this will often appear in person specifications or competency frameworks; when working in an educational environment there may be course learning outcomes, level descriptors, competency frameworks or subject benchmark statements.

You then need to identify where there are training needs, knowledge and skills gaps. This may be based on strategic plans, interviews with senior staff (such as managers or tutors), survey information, existing data (such as usage figures or data on plagiarism cases) or external reviews. You will usually need to build up your own evidence base from questionnaires and interviews. Cross-check the information you get from these sources as individuals may over- or underestimate their expertise or think that they understand processes or systems when they only have a superficial knowledge.

Boydell and Leary (1996) offer a detailed discussion of TNA and emphasize its scale, stressing it requires process, relationship and content management skills. Williamson (1993) is a very accessible and practical starting point. There is also a helpful guide from the UK's Chartered Institute of Personnel and Development (CIPD).

✓ BEST FOR

- working in organizations
- systematic programme linked to staff development
- meeting the needs of learners and organizations.

+ MORE

- Run part of the TNA online rather than by using paper questionnaires or face-to-face interviews.

! WATCH OUT

- Always cross-check findings with other sources and be careful to match any gaps that you find in training and skills against organizational goals.
- It is tempting to skip on the analysis before designing teaching, but it is the only way of ensuring that the learning best meets the needs of the individual and/or organization.

➤ REFERENCES

Boydell, T. and Leary, M. (1996) *Identifying Training Needs, Training Essentials*, Chartered Institute of Personnel and Development (CIPD).

CIPD *Identifying Learning and Talent Development Needs*, http://www.cipd.co.uk/hr-resources/factsheets/identifying-learning-talent-development-needs.aspx.

Williamson, M. (1993) *Training Needs Analysis*, Library Training Guides, Library Association Publishing.

4 Learner analysis

A Training Needs Analysis (TNA) is a strategic tool usually mapped to organizational (or curriculum) needs, whereas a learner analysis is focused on the learners who will actually be attending your teaching sessions. A TNA may strongly influence the 'what' of your teaching, but the learner analysis will influence the 'how'. (In some contexts your sessions can be purely learner-driven in which case the needs of the learners are paramount.)

A common model for instructional design – the ADDIE model – begins with Analysis, thus emphasizing its importance in underpinning teaching and training:

- Analysis
- Design
- Development
- Implementation
- Evaluation.

This model is useful to remember when beginning to plan teaching, as the Analysis stage is often forgotten – this involves reflection on the 'variables' discussed in **A framework for designing and delivering teaching and learning**. The model ends with Evaluation and it is important to acknowledge that these two stages often involve the same processes, with Evaluation usually feeding into the Analysis for future teaching.

There are many factors to consider in the Analysis and Design stages – it is a good idea to use a planning form to help remember everything (see **Lesson planning** for an example).

Questions to ask about your learners:

- What knowledge will they already have? Match this to the prerequisites of your session. You may need to suggest pre-course reading or attendance on another session as a prerequisite. (See **Mixed abilities**.)

- What fears might they have? This enables you to plan how to address these fears – it may be that you need to provide reassurance that the session won't be too 'techy' or that it won't be a waste of their time.
- What do they want to know? What is important to them? While you may have set learning outcomes to achieve, it is helpful to try and make this as relevant as you can to your learners by linking to something they may want or need to find out about.
- What is their motivation? What might their approach to learning be? Deep, surface or strategic? (See **Motivation**.)
- What are their learning styles? Every learner is different and may prefer to learn in different ways. You should consider this when designing activities and materials in order to maximize the opportunities for learning. (See **Learning styles**.)
- Do they have any special requirements? This may be in terms of access to the teaching room, dietary requirements if you're providing catering, or requirements in terms of teaching materials. (See **Inclusion**.)
- What are their cultural references? When choosing appropriate examples or images to include in your materials, you should consider whether they are appropriate. (See **Cultural relevance** and **Jokes and humour**.)
- What level of autonomy do they have? Are the learners used to planning their own learning or do they expect to receive detailed instruction from a teacher? The level of support each learner requires will vary – you will usually need to provide more support at the start before they are confident enough to carry out tasks on their own. (See **Facilitating learning**.)
- What are their experiences of education? Your learners will be influenced by previous experiences of learning which you will need to consider. For example, learners in the workplace or community may have uncomfortable memories of formal education so this may lead to anxiety; or school leavers may not be used to the new expectations that higher education will bring and will need to be supported.

✓ BEST FOR

- all sessions
- matching teaching and learning techniques and delivery to learners' needs.

✚ MORE

- If you are lucky enough to have access to your learners before your sessions, you can find out this information and tailor sessions for specific groups. If not, you could incorporate techniques at the start of your session to find this out (see **Pre-session audit**). In any case, you could create a model of a typical learner to plan your sessions (based on prior experience or discussion with those who may know more about the learners) and adapt delivery on the day.

❓ WATCH OUT

- While it is good practice to consider individual needs, in practice this is not always possible, particularly in group sessions. Design a range of activities and do your best to adapt to individual needs during the session.

5 Pre-session audit

Knowing your learners is a key part of the planning process but one that we do not always have the luxury of having. Information literacy teaching is often a one-off event delivered to learners of whom we have no prior knowledge and who we may not see again. This means that we might need to make guesses at prior knowledge, experience and motivations of learners when preparing sessions. However, there are things that we can do to help:

- Ask the other stakeholders – these could be teachers, lecturers, societies or individuals involved in arranging the learning and teaching event. Concentrate on finding out what the learners know already and what they need. The latter is easier to find out than the former, as those booking your teaching may not know about the learners' prior experience of information skills. Try to ask more than one individual and triangulate – for example, in a school, college or university you might want to talk to teacher/lecturers about what the learners need and also IT or media technicians about their experience or observation of the group.
- Ask the learners. This can be by prior arrangement – sending out pre-session questionnaires could be useful but be careful with your questions as people will often under- or overestimate their expertise or knowledge. Alternatively these questions could be asked on a session booking form (if used). Try to ask specific questions rather than asking learners to rank themselves. Ask for qualitative answers rather than tick box or ranking scales.
- If pre-session questions to the learners or their sponsors are not possible or appropriate, then make a point of asking the learners as they join your teaching session. Position yourself near to the doorway or chat as you wait for latecomers. Do not interrogate but ask friendly, targeted questions as people arrive. This means that you will need to be flexible with your planning – there is no point ploughing on with something if they have told you that they already know it or it is apparent that it is irrelevant.

- Ask directly what your learners want from the event and then incorporate this into a revised set of learning outcomes.
- If you are working with a reasonably small group, introductions can be a good way to gather some extra information about your learners. You may wish to ask what their favourite information sources are (do they use anything other than Google?) and ask if there is anything specific they want to get out of the session. The answers to these questions can help you gauge knowledge and experience, although be prepared for the fact that some learners may talk too much and others may not say anything at all.
- Build in a quiz or activity at the start of the session – this will actively engage learners from the start, and also help you gauge their knowledge and ability.

However you find out about your learners, it is important that you use the information discovered in your planning. This may sound obvious but the temptation to deliver what you think that they want rather than that which you find they need, can be difficult to overcome. Remember that no matter what you plan for, you always need to be flexible.

✓ BEST FOR

- All teachers should attempt to audit their learners in some way.

✚ MORE

- Use feedback from similar groups to inform the planning of the next session.

❗ WATCH OUT

- If you ask questions then be sure to use the answers (or explain why you will not be doing so). Learners will often not realize that they do not know something, so make your questions specific to both the session and the learners, rather than general questions about how much the learners do know.
- It is very frustrating to be asked about what you know already and want from the session, see your answers recorded and then witness the session

continue without any appreciable application of those answers. Even if you do not want to vary too much from your plan, draw in your learners' experiences – and emphasize when you are addressing the issues and questions they have raised.

6 Learning styles

Learning styles relate to the idea that individuals prefer to learn in different ways. The value, or even the existence, of learning styles is a deeply controversial subject. Many psychologists challenge the validity of much learning styles theory, arguing that an understanding of individual learning differences does not in fact lead to any significantly beneficial impact on learning. Equally, others argue that by understanding learning styles we can enhance the effectiveness of learning.

There are many different learning styles theories, including Kolb's experiential learning model (Kolb, 1984) and adapted by Honey and Mumford (1982), and Fleming's VARK model (2001–10; detailed below). Learning styles theories are linked to discussions of personality and individual difference, including theories of multiple intelligence (having a musical intelligence, for example). Critics of learning styles theory suggest that there is limited evidence of their actual impact – see Revell (2005), Coffield (2004) and Hargreaves et al. (2005).

In practice we suggest a gentle, pragmatic compromise. An awareness of learning styles and their application is a good way to direct your focus to the learner, and to develop your appreciation that people learn things in different ways. It is important not to make assumptions about your learners (such as 'all art students are visual learners'), or explicitly categorize learners based on your knowledge of them (labelling them).

Be prepared for different learning styles by creating a variety of routes into your teaching – this can be as simple as some verbal input from you, a written handout or reading list, diagrammatic explanations of concepts and some activity-based learning. Including a variety of activities that cater to different learning styles will also reduce the potential for learners to become lost, distracted or bored.

The two dominant expressions of learning styles are those by Kolb and VARK. It is not the purpose of this book to go into detail (see the references for a more extensive discussion) but they do share some key elements:

- Kolb describes for four types of learner: those that prefer reflection, activity, practical outcomes or theory. You can then apply a range of learning and teaching interventions to best match this variety.

- VARK has four (different) types of learner:
  - Visual learners prefer graphics, mind maps, posters and pictures.
  - Auditory learners prefer using podcasts, listening games, group work and discussion.
  - Read/write learners create opportunities for note-taking and writing on flip charts.
  - Kinaesthetic learners prefer activity-based learning, opportunities to move around the room or space, and role-play.

Although an awareness of learning styles is useful to understanding learners and the learning process, ultimately the only solution to group teaching is to build in a variety of activities. Learners should be encouraged to find their own learning style and develop appropriate studying techniques. Remember, it may be fine to be a visual learner, but if you are studying a text-based subject, you still need to engage with text. It is the responsibility of those teaching to develop full-rounded learners, who are able to draw from a range of learning modalities where necessary.

✓ BEST FOR

- This is a useful underpinning approach that can help you, as a teacher, to understand learner diversity.

✚ MORE

- Learning styles will change with the task and circumstance, although you will retain a dominant one. Be flexible.
- Realizing that people learn in different ways can also help you understand why you get some critical feedback: sometimes things are your fault, sometimes it might be the learner, sometimes just circumstance.

❢ WATCH OUT

- Do not let worrying about learning styles dominate your planning – as long as you are flexible and varied in your delivery then it should not be an issue.
- Be careful that you do not impose your own learning style on your

learners – be flexible enough to accept that some learners will need a different emphasis. Test yourself in one of the many online quizzes and map your preferred style onto your teaching.

◆ REFERENCES

Coffield, F. et al. (2004) *Learning Styles and Pedagogy in Post-16 Learning: a systematic and critical review*, Learning and Skills Research Centre.

Fleming, N. (2001–10) *VARK: a guide to learning styles*, www.vark-learn.com.

Hargreaves, D. et al. (2005) *About Learning: report of the learning working group*, Demos.

Honey, P. and Mumford, A. (1982) *The Manual of Learning Styles*, Peter Honey Publications.

Kolb, D. (1984) *Experiential Learning*, Prentice Hall.

Revell, P. (2005) Each to their own, *Guardian*, 31 May, www.guardian.co.uk/education/2005/may/31/schools.uk3.

7 Facilitating learning

Remember, that for learning to take place some form of catalyst is usually required. Humans do not absorb all knowledge simply by a process of osmosis. That catalyst may be an event, or a change in learner circumstance, but most often a learning and teaching event and a teacher will create that opportunity. Your role as teacher/trainer/facilitator will shape the learning experience in your session – the activities used and your own behaviour will affect the end result.

The nature of learning is still the focus for much academic discussion, but rather than summarize huge amounts of current debate, we will focus here on some key issues and themes.

Fundamentally, you must always remember that learning takes place at different levels and in different ways. In order to maximize the impact of your learning and teaching work, you need to have a clear idea of what you are trying to achieve in your session and design your learning activities to reach these aims.

Bloom's taxonomy of learning (1956) is a framework that can be used to help guide your thinking about how you want your learners to progress and develop. Bloom's taxonomy has three domains: the cognitive (relating to knowledge), the affective (values and beliefs) and the psychomotor (physical skills). These relate to 'knowledge, attitude and skills' structures which you may see underpinning many approaches to learning and evaluation.

Each domain has a series of levels that act as 'building blocks' for learning. Information literacy sessions are likely to involve all three domains, but will normally focus on the cognitive domain – the acquisition and use of knowledge. The psychomotor domain involves things like use of a keyboard and mouse and ability to navigate websites. The affective domain is often a key part of introductory sessions where the librarian may be trying to change the learners' views of the library – seeing it as a more valuable resource, or changing the learners' perceptions of the value of information skills (how many learners are often overly confident in their information skills, feeling they have little to learn?) or even in helping to overcome the learners' own negative perceptions of whether it is right and appropriate for them to be in a library.

Diagram **7.1** shows the levels within Bloom's cognitive domain and some verbs that can be used to describe how this can be demonstrated (ideal for use in designing activities and assessments):

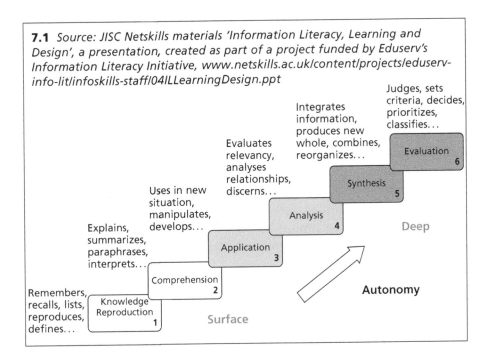

7.1 *Source: JISC Netskills materials 'Information Literacy, Learning and Design', a presentation, created as part of a project funded by Eduserv's Information Literacy Initiative, www.netskills.ac.uk/content/projects/eduserv-info-lit/infoskills-staff/04ILLearningDesign.ppt*

With information literacy teaching, you will normally want to guide your student to the higher levels of Bloom's taxonomy, beyond simply memorizing and repeating information to evaluating and synthesizing information. It should be noted that evaluation appears in two contexts in the model – firstly at the Analysis level, where the traditional information literacy activity of 'evaluating information' would take place. Secondly, the Evaluation level of the model relates to the learner's ability to evaluate and determine their own information and knowledge acquisition and use – ultimately the highest level goal of information literacy teaching: creating the 'independent' learner.

Remember that the learning that takes place at the lower levels is still vital – this provides the foundation for higher-level learning. It is important to understand that your activities need to match the level of learning you want to achieve – there are many examples of courses being taught at high levels, where the assessments are simply asking for information reproduction and thus demonstrating only lower-level learning.

At the lower levels, teaching activities may include simply transmitting information to learners, whether by a lecture, podcast, handout or online resource. You will usually find that in order for learners to progress, some kind of interaction (known as a 'transaction') needs to take place between the teacher and learner (or between the learners themselves). This may involve questions, tests or activities. In order to reach the highest levels of learning, the knowledge needs to be 'transformed' by each individual learner – this means that the learner must understand for themselves and make their own sense and meaning of the knowledge. As a teacher, you can guide learners to this point through questioning to encourage reflection. At various points in your teaching, you may be involving transmission, transaction and transformation and your role may move from knowledge presenter to facilitator to advisor (Ecclestone, 2000).

The 'Blooming Blooms' activity used at Kilmacolm Nursery by Katrina Little is a good example of mapping questions to the various levels of Bloom's taxonomy, which can be applied no matter what the age of the learner (see reference below and example included in **Questions** tip).

✓ BEST FOR

- planning teaching activities
- ensuring activities are matched to appropriate learning outcomes.

✚ MORE

- Think about techniques you have come across in various teaching situations and consider what is actually happening during these sessions:
  - Is information simply being transmitted? Anything that simply involves listening or reading information is transmission – your learners will either remember or they won't, but as a teacher using these methods alone you will never know.
  - Is there any interaction between the learner and teacher?
  - Are your assessments/quizzes simply asking for information to be reproduced and repeated back to you? Most learning involves some core knowledge that must be memorized but for learning to become 'deep' it must go beyond simple memory and become internalized through understanding.

— Are your hands-on tasks simply asking for users to follow step-by-step instructions? While this behaviourist technique is useful for learners to learn a particular procedure, you must ensure they can replicate this themselves, through some kind of assessment.

— How are you encouraging learners to reflect on their own experiences in order to make connections for themselves? Scaffolded techniques, where you provide a framework for learning, are ideal for this – do not give away all the answers, but provide a framework to enable learners to find the answers themselves. The amount of scaffolding you need to provide to will depend on your learners.

? WATCH OUT

- Remember that despite everything you do as a teacher, the learner's own motivation is central to successful learning. Phil Race (2009) places 'motivation' at the centre of his model of learning. So in the end, if the learners don't want to learn, they won't. However, you can try to nurture learner motivation through engaging activities and teaching techniques, alongside your own enthusiasm and ensuring your sessions are relevant to their needs.
- The same principles apply when designing online learning activities. Think carefully about what is actually being achieved in your online activities – a polished online tutorial may actually only be providing low-level learning through information transmission.
- Ensure your online learning activities match your learner analysis – often teachers expect too much (or not enough!) of their learners in the online environment. For example, if your learners would need close facilitation in a face-to-face session, then don't expect them to be more independent online – they will still need your support.

⦿ REFERENCES

Bloom, B. S. (1956) *Taxonomy of Educational Objectives, Handbook I: the cognitive domain*, David McKay Co. Inc.

Ecclestone, K. (2000) Assessment and Critical Autonomy in Post-compulsory Education in the UK, *Journal of Education and Work*, **13** (2), 141–62.

Irvine, C. (2010) *Questioning – Kilmacolm's Innovative Blooming Blooms approach*, National Information Literacy Framework Scotland case study, http://caledonianblogs.net/nilfs/2010/02/25/questioning-kilmacolms-innovative-blooming-blooms-approach/

JISC Netskills (n.d.) *Teaching Information Skills: materials for secondary schools,* www.netskills.ac.uk/content/projects/eduserv-info-lit/infoskills-materials.html

Race, P. (2009) *'Ripples' Model of Learning: seven factors underpinning successful learning,* http://phil-race.co.uk/most-popular-downloads.

Acknowledgement

Many thanks to JISC Netskills for permission to include their material in this tip.

8 Aims

The aim of any session clarifies the overall goal of your teaching in a clear and unambiguous way. Without it you cannot set learning objectives or outcomes because these should flow naturally from the aim (or sometimes you may have multiple aims). The aim can be set by you – and amended after contact with the learners – or it may be set by an external person or agency. For example, a lecturer may ask you to improve the referencing skills of his or her class. This would set the aim of the session but the learning outcomes from that would perhaps cover plagiarism, and specific ways to reference journals, books, websites, and so on.

Useful words to use in setting aims include: *know, understand, determine, appreciate*. These are much broader, even aspirational, than those that you would use for learning outcomes, as the latter need to be assessed. If the learning outcomes that apply to achieving aims can be assessed then it follows that you will be able to assess whether the overall aim has been achieved. (See **Learning outcomes**.)

For example, a broad aim may be 'to use Google effectively', but a specific learning outcome may be 'to carry out a phrase search' or 'to be able to refine a search using the minus sign'.

Always communicate the aim of any session to the learners – they should know what they are there to achieve and be able to comment on it. Clearly stating the aims and learning outcomes on all publicity for your session should help ensure learners attend the appropriate course and have realistic expectations.

✓ BEST FOR

- clearly articulating the aim of your teaching session and communicating it to the learners
- clarifying the scope of your session
- managing learners' expectations.

✚ MORE

- You may find that, as you plan a session in detail, your learning outcomes or objectives start to move outside the remit of the original aim. All learning outcomes should stem from, and contribute towards achieving, the aim. If you are moving outside of the aim then either change the aim or re-focus your learning outcomes.
- You do not need to articulate the aim of a session by saying: 'The aim of this session is . . .' Instead, you can just state the aim of the lesson: 'Today we will look at referencing.'

❗ WATCH OUT

- Try not to make your aim(s) too specific – the learning outcomes should specify how you will meet the aim in detail. However, they should not be so wide that they cannot be achieved within the time and resources that you have available. Especially when starting out, many of us try to fill sessions with too much content in a desire to be as comprehensive as possible in a one-shot teaching session. We do this both in order to cover all possible learning needs and questions and also through a lack of experience in knowing what the key learning points should actually be. Experience, peer observation and feedback from learners will all help you to focus on the key learning points.

9 Learning outcomes

Every teaching session should have clear aims and outcomes. An aim is usually defined in broad terms, whereas outcomes are the specific skills or knowledge that learners will achieve or develop.

In recent years, there has been a trend towards 'learning outcomes' as opposed to 'teaching objectives', that is, thinking more about what the learner can do by the end of the session, rather than what you want to teach them. An easy way to ensure your outcomes are learner-focused is to start by saying: 'By the end of the session you will be able to...'

It is usually desirable to ensure that your outcomes are measurable: can the learner show that they have achieved the outcome? This is useful for gathering evidence of the impact of your teaching, as well as providing the learner with a sense of achievement. Learning outcomes are therefore closely tied to assessment and evaluation and you should consider how you will measure outcomes right at the start.

With information skills teaching, many of your outcomes may be to raise awareness of library resources rather than impart specific skills.

✓ BEST FOR

- setting a clear scope for your session
- ensuring your learners know exactly what will be covered in the session.

+ MORE

- Make sure your learning outcomes are clearly stated on any promotional material and at the start of the session as this will help to manage your learners' expectations.
- Be careful about trying to achieve too much in one session. A rough guide would be no more than two or three outcomes for an hour of teaching.
- When writing learning outcomes be careful about the wording you

choose. Some outcomes ask for repetition of information and will not require understanding or analysis. For example, asking learners to 'list', 'state' or 'describe' will lead to information reproduction, whereas 'compare', 'justify' or 'defend' require higher-level thought. (See **Facilitating learning** for more detail on levels of learning.)

- It is very easy to write outcomes that are hard to measure. For example, any that begin with 'to understand' or 'to appreciate' are difficult to assess (these would be more appropriate for **Aims**). It is better to rephrase the outcome so that understanding can be shown by explaining, comparing, demonstrating, and so on.

⁇ WATCH OUT

- Remember to refer back to the learning outcomes throughout your planning – you should not be doing anything that fails to, in some way, contribute to achieving the learning outcome.

10 Assessment

There are many different forms of assessment, ranging from the formal examination to simple observation. Some of the most effective ways to assess information literacy are discussed as separate tips in this book. It is important to remember that assessment is an essential part of the learning experience as it is the most effective way of ensuring that your learners actually learn what you have been teaching them. Assessed tasks or activities are often the most effective way that learners start to internalize and understand the information with which they have been provided, or to put it another way, assessment turns information into personal knowledge.

Assessment is not always about exams and tests. Instead, think of it as a catch-all description for the process of letting the learners try out and demonstrate what they have learnt.

When planning assessment ask yourself three questions:

- What do I want to measure?
- Is this the best way to assess?
- Is what I am testing important or significant?

When planning your teaching, you need to think about how to check that the learning outcomes have been achieved. This can be done in a variety of ways, but you need to link your aims, objectives and learning outcomes to the assessment to make it most effective.

There are different kinds of assessment:

- Summative assessment takes place at the conclusion of the learning experience.
- Formative assessment takes place during the learning experience and can be something as simple as asking your learners to do a task and giving them feedback while they are working on it.
- Diagnostic assessment takes place prior to your sessions and can be

used to assess existing knowledge and ability to inform your teaching and to benchmark learning.

Remember that all assessment tasks and activities should have the following five qualities:

1 **Validity**
   Assessment should test the learning outcomes. It is also good practice to select tasks relevant and appropriate to the process. So, for example, setting a bibliography task would be a good activity for students needing to demonstrate literature searching, reviewing, and referencing skills, but perhaps not a suitable activity for family historians who would rather demonstrate their searching skills by drawing up a genealogy. This can be quite difficult to achieve as after all, it can be easier to test recall ('Do you know how many books you can borrow?') via a quiz than understanding.

2 **Reliability**
   A good assessment task or activity needs to be reliable in testing the specified learning outcomes objectively on more than one occasion and by more than one teacher. You can ensure this by drawing up assessment criteria and, if necessary, a marking scheme or plan.

3 **Efficiency**
   Assessment should make good use of the teacher's and learner's time: for example, it may not be helpful to set an assessment task that takes ages to set up, perhaps requiring the learner to register to use a system, go through an induction process and then be assessed on a very short online activity.

4 **Fairness**
   You should ensure that the assessment is fair, not just by avoiding random outcomes that mean that you will fail anyway even if you do everything right, but also by checking that you do not accidentally exclude or disadvantage some of your learners. Be careful of using culturally inappropriate examples, making the assessment too difficult or excluding learners who are disabled or who have specific learning differences.

5 **Value**
   You need to set assessments that the learners will value. This usually means setting assessments that are relevant, interesting and challenging to the learners and which match the aims and objectives that you have set.

✓ BEST FOR

- all learning activities.

✚ MORE

- See the tips on **Self-assessment**, **Peer assessment**, **Bibliographies** and **Quizzes** for specific examples of assessment types. Think about ways you can use technology to make the assessment more dynamic, for example, using personal response systems, using a social bookmarking site to explore tagging, or creating shared bibliographies on some of the many reference management sites.
- See example **10.1** for a sample assignment brief used with second-year university biomedical science students.

❗ WATCH OUT

- First of all, make sure that you have followed the five principles described above. It is possible to design efficient assessments that are not valued. Some online assessments can be particularly prone to this: reflect about how often you start an online survey or quiz and give up because it is too long, too boring or just pointless.
- Secondly, remember that assessment is part of the learning and teaching process, not its purpose. Sometimes you can focus too much on teaching to the assessment task, rather than designing the assessment to meet the aims and objectives of your learning and teaching event. This reduces both the validity and value of assessment.
- Thirdly, involvement in assessment can be administratively complex and sometimes politically delicate, especially if there is a summative element. This can be for all sorts of reasons. If you are involved in summative assessment, your learners will be concerned about their performance. You may find that you are dealing with people who want extended deadlines, provide mitigating circumstances (about which you may need to decide whether they are acceptable) or who even pressure you about their grades. You also need to be conscious of the rules and regulations that apply to your assessment. These may be internal rules or those set by an awarding body. There can also be challenges to status. Library and information professionals may not be perceived as suitably qualified or of sufficient/appropriate status to be involved in assessment. There are

10.1 *Sample assignment used at De Montfort University with 2nd year Biomedical Sciences students*

Library and Information Skills 2009–10

HAND-IN: Friday 20 November, 12 noon, to the Student Advice Centre
TUTOR'S NAME:

This assignment tests the following areas of skills and knowledge:

- searching skills, especially in relation to databases
- ability to select appropriate keywords, sources and resources
- referencing and bibliography.

You are required to do the following:

1. Select one of the following topics and include this on your submission:

    a. What are the dangers of prescription-only medicine and addiction?
    b. Can acupuncture cure migraines?
    c. What can be done to combat the high level of heart disease in the UK?
    d. Should we pay more for health care?

2. Select appropriate keywords and sources (such as databases, web resources, etc.) that you will use to research your topic and present these either as lists or mind maps. (10 marks) Write a short summary of why you chose the keywords selected and why you chose to search the sources you have identified (maximum 150 words). (25 marks)
3. Produce a critical annotated bibliography of 10–15 items (books, journal articles, websites and any other sources covered in the library sessions) about your topic. Each item in the bibliography should be correctly cited in the Harvard style and annotated to show why you have selected it. (40 marks)
4. Write a short summary of how effective the sources and keywords you identified were in producing appropriate results and whether you needed to amend your search (maximum 150 words). (25 marks)

Your keywords and sources used should be appropriate to the chosen topic and each item on your bibliography should be:

- current and relevant to your topic
- referenced correctly according to the Harvard system.

All assignments need to be word-processed and handed in to the Student Advice Centre by 12 noon on Friday 20 November. **Late assignments will be penalized**.

5. Support material
The following library publications will help you with your assignment:

How to Find Journals and Journal Articles
How to Undertake a Literature Search and Review
The Harvard System of Referencing.

These are all available both in print from the library and online at: www.library.dmu.ac.uk/Support/Guides.

examples in educational institutions (schools, colleges and universities) where librarians have done all the teaching and designed the assessment but are not allowed to mark the work because they are not academic staff.

→ FURTHER READING

Dunn, L. et al. (2004) *The Student Assessment Handbook*, RoutledgeFalmer.

11 Reflection

Reflection ensures learning becomes deeper and longer lasting. Many people tend not to think too much about their information sources or their strategies for finding information, simply 'getting by' using information sources they are familiar with (increasingly, learners rely solely on Google). Reflection is also a vital part of becoming an independent learner; therefore, encouraging reflection is a major aim of most information literacy teaching.

Reflection is included in some models of information literacy. For example, the outcomes for the Association of College and Research Libraries (ACRL) Information Literacy Competency, Standard Four ('The information literate student, individually or as a member of a group, uses information effectively to accomplish a specific purpose'), include:

- maintains a journal or log of activities related to the information seeking, evaluating, and communicating process
- reflects on past successes, failures, and alternative strategies.

Christine Bruce (2004) argues that the following is required to become information literate:

- experiencing information literacy (learning)
- reflection on experience (being aware of learning)
- application of experience to novel contexts (transfer of learning).

Reflection is integral to the learning process, and enabling learners to become effective reflectors contributes to their ability to become lifelong learners. If a learner is able to reflect on their information seeking and identify how to improve in the future, they are more able to work independently.

Time for reflection should be built in to any face-to-face teaching sessions you run. If you are in the position to set assignments for learners, tasks can be set to encourage reflective writing.

✓ BEST FOR

- most learning and teaching.

✚ MORE

- Reflection is not just about describing or retelling experiences. Although that may be the starting point, it should move on to more personal comments and interpretation.
- Encourage reflection in your sessions by creating an open environment where learners feel able to ask questions and give comments.
- Relate new learning to prior experience.
- Although reflection is often done at the end of an information-seeking task, it can also be encouraged during the process to review and adapt search strategies.
- Questions to encourage reflective thinking:
  — What did you like/not like about a resource?
  — Which techniques worked/did not work for you?
  — Which techniques did you find hard/easy to use?
  — How will this improve your searching in future?
  — Speculative questions: 'What if…?'
- Questions to avoid:
  — Closed questions, such as those that can only have a very short or yes/no answer.
  — Leading questions (such as: 'Do you think your search wasn't successful because the keywords you chose were too broad?'). However, if the learner is really struggling to identify issues themselves, leading questions may be appropriate.

❗ WATCH OUT

- Bear in mind that many people are not used to reflecting on their experiences and may need guidance. It can be helpful to prepare a writing frame – a template with suitable headings for prompts.

↔ REFERENCES

ACRL (2011) *Information Literacy Competence Standards for Higher Education*, www.ftrf.org/ala/mgrps/divs/acrl/standards/informationliteracycompetency.cfm#stan.

Bruce, C. (2004) *Australian and New Zealand Information Literacy Framework: principles, standards and practice*, 2nd edn, p. 7, http://archive.caul.edu.au/info-literacy/InfoLiteracyFramework.pdf.

12 Evaluation

Evaluation should be an integral part of any teaching or training. Evaluation will let you know whether your learners have achieved the intended learning outcomes and it is an opportunity to gather evidence of the impact of your teaching sessions. Evaluation and assessment are closely linked.

Methods of evaluation should be considered when developing teaching and embedded throughout the teaching process, not just bolted on to the end of a session. Evaluation is often thought of as the printed form handed out at the end of courses, but it should be a much more considered process that is integral to your planning, development and delivery. Take every opportunity to gather evidence of the impact of your teaching.

Evaluation can take place on different levels. Although designed for the business context, Kirkpatrick's (1959) four levels of evaluation model is widely used. The levels are:

1 **Reaction**

This is how the learner *feels* at the end of your teaching session or course. It is usually measured by the 'happy sheet', so named as it can really only measure at the reaction level. This is an opportunity to gather learners' opinions on your session, including practicalities such as organization, venue, refreshments, etc., but also on content – did they feel the session was useful? Did the session meet its aims? This can also be a good opportunity to find out what further training is needed. You can attempt to measure beyond reaction by asking how learners will use the knowledge and/or skills gained in the session.

2 **Learning**

This relates to knowledge or skills acquisition – what did the learners actually learn? This is where evaluation is closely linked to assessment. This does not necessarily mean formal assessment via an exam, etc., but could be informal questioning by the teacher or a demonstration of skills in a practical session. In your planning, think about how learners can demonstrate that they have learned what you are trying to teach – this should impact the design of your session.

3 **Behaviour**

This evaluates whether your teaching or training has actually translated into a change in behaviour for the learner (the application of the learning). This is harder to evaluate, as you may no longer have contact with the learner to witness a behavioural change. If you have regular teaching sessions with the same group then this is easier to assess. You could send out post-session evaluation to try to assess longer-term impact. Alternatively, you could look for evidence of impact elsewhere, for example, is there a correlation between use of library services/databases and those who have attended your sessions? Bear in mind that there may be data protection issues in accessing this type of information.

4 **Result**

This level evaluates whether the change in behaviour has had any impact on results. In Kirkpatrick's original context this would be improved business results; in an educational context, this could be exam results – for example, any correlation between use of library resources and improved exam results. 'Results' may be harder to define for information literacy teaching in other contexts. One issue with measuring results is that it becomes harder to prove the direct cause of a particular result as there may be many several factors involved.

✓ BEST FOR

- identifying areas for improvement
- gathering evidence of the impact of your sessions
- knowing whether your sessions have achieved their aims
- identifying further topics for delivery.

+ MORE

- Set some short quizzes throughout the session, asking how it is going. This can be especially effective when using technology-enhanced learning.
- Place cards on each person's chair with prompts to gather feedback. Make this quick and simple, for example: 'Which one thing will you take away today?' or 'What would you like further training on?'

- Use the Stop, Start, Continue technique described in **Stop, Start, Continue feedback**.
- A couple of days after the session, e-mail learners a link to a page where they can provide online feedback. This allows them time for reflection.
- Some of the best feedback comes from observing your learners' body language: is it closed (crossed arms and legs) or open? Are they responding to you, or are they staring out of the window or doodling?
- Use a teaching log or diary to record your own thoughts and reflections on how the session or event went. This could include reflections on the specific event and how to improve content and delivery, but may also include reflections on your own performance and development needs.

❗ WATCH OUT

- You should only collect the data if you are going to use it. Ask questions that will improve your performance and the learning experience. For example, it is pointless asking whether your voice projects went well after the first couple of times unless you have taken action to correct the situation (such as by using a microphone or taking some vocal training).

➽ REFERENCE

Kirkpatrick, D. L. (1959) *Evaluating Training Programs*, 2nd edn, Berrett-Koehler.

13 Social learning

Most learning and teaching approaches discussed in this book derive from Alfred Bandura's principles of social learning or related theories (1977).

Social learning proposes that people learn through observing the behaviour, attitudes and the related outcomes of others. It emphasizes a dialogue rather than transmission in the transfer of knowledge, and from our perspective we should recognize that the dialogue is not merely between teacher and learner, but between the individual and the environment as a whole. As well as being important in our own teaching, social learning reinforces the importance of modelling good learning behaviours and attitudes throughout our interactions with others. Social learning also provides effective learning design and assessment.

There are some basic social learning concepts:

- People can learn through observation. This can be positive or negative – watching poor behaviour can lead to bad behaviour in others, be that violence or research skills!
- Mental states are important to learning.
- Learning does not necessarily lead to a change in behaviour; or rather people can learn new information without demonstrating new behaviours.

In order to make social learning effective, the following elements are required:

- **Attention**. In order to learn, you need to be paying attention. Anything that detracts your attention is going to have a negative effect on observational learning. If the teaching is interesting or there is a novel aspect to the situation, you are far more likely to dedicate your full attention to learning.
- **Retention**. The ability to store information is also an important part of the learning process. Retention can be affected by a number of factors, but remember that practical application of the learning can be especially effective.

- **Reproduction**. Once you have paid attention to the model and retained the information, it is time to actually perform the behaviour you observed. Further practice of the learned behaviour leads to improvement and skill advancement. In this book, we suggest that this is most often achieved through assessment.
- **Motivation**. Finally, in order for observational learning to be successful, you have to be motivated to imitate the behaviour you have seen. It is suggested that reinforcement and punishment play an important role in motivation – think of the latter more in the terms of 'not rewarding bad behaviour', so not allowing poor timekeeping, or letting people get away with not completing activities.

Social learning theory has sometimes been called a bridge between behaviourist and cognitive learning theories because it encompasses attention, memory and motivation.

✓ BEST FOR

- These theories can be applied in most learning contexts.

✚ MORE

- This is a framework, so can be applied very flexibly and as required.
- The model of 'Attention, Retention, Reproduction, Motivation' can be used as a checklist for your learning activities.

❗ WATCH OUT

Two problems in particular:

- introducing too much 'social' in the social learning
- engineering elegant social learning strategies but letting the pedagogic design overwhelm the learning outcomes.

❧ REFERENCE

Bandura, A. (1977) *Social Learning Theory*, General Learning Press.

14 Lesson planning

Session or lesson plans are useful in preparing a teaching session, during its delivery, assisting you in reflection and review, and in creating a usable record of content and design of learning and teaching opportunities. Lesson plans can help ensure that the many factors outlined in the first tip (**A framework for designing teaching and learning**) are addressed.

Lesson plans normally outline the aims and outcomes of the session, describe the learning activities to be used and provide a timetable and structure for the session. The plans are a valuable resource for you, but remember they can also be shared with colleagues who may run the same session, provide a formal record of good practice or be the basis of your teaching log. (See **Evaluation.**)

There are several approaches to lesson planning. At the most minimal level, a lesson plan might be just a timetable. More helpfully, draw up a simple table, perhaps looking something like example **14.1**:

14.1				
Learning outcome	**Activity**	**Time**	**Material**	**Assessment**
To be able to use a recognized referencing format (such as Harvard) for citing books, journals, websites and other formats	Referencing exercise	20 minutes	Samples of material Harvard referencing guide Student worksheet	Peer assessment using model answers

A lesson plan in this format is an essential tool for planning and structuring a learning and teaching event, often giving you a clearer picture of the shape of what you want to do. The plan can serve as a helpful prompt in reviewing session design and can record how you are integrating inputs, activities and assessment.

Lesson plans can be much more extensive. In this format, they are commonly used by schoolteachers and there are many free lesson plans available on the internet (try the Guardian Teacher Network, http://teachers.guardian.co.uk/?CMP=KNCJOBTXT3828). Most school lesson plans will state how they relate to the curriculum. This may not be as easy to define for information literacy tasks outside formal education, but you can cross-reference your learning outcomes against one of the information literacy standards discussed in **Information literacy and standards**. If you can map your sessions to a curriculum or subject standard then this will help promote the relevance of your teaching to teachers and academics. Example **14.2** shows a sample planning form.

14.2 *JISC Netskills Information Literacy Lesson Planning Form, www.netskills.ac.uk/content/projects/eduserv-info-lit/infoskills-staff/12ILLessonPlanningForm.doc*

Title and duration of session

Aim and learning outcomes

What is the broad aim or goal and what are the specific learning outcomes for this task? Think about which level of Bloom's taxonomy of learning they map to. Is there progression in your outcomes? (Remember progression can be planned within a session as well as across a number of sessions as part of a programme.)

Relevance to curriculum

Which areas of the curriculum does this activity support?

Continued on next page

14.2 *Continued*

Information literacy (IL) area(s) covered

Refer to your chosen IL model or framework

Teaching methods and activities

Think about what approach is appropriate for your session based on the type of learning you are trying to achieve. What activities will you use? How will the approach change as learners progress through the activities?

Remember – transmission, transaction and transformation. What information or facts do they need to know? Will you do a presentation or handout? Can you get them to find the information themselves in a transactional and creative way? E.g. games, treasure hunts. What tasks or questions can you set to deepen learning? Your questions may guide students to a desired answer, but allow them to reach conclusions themselves. Will you ask them to reflect on the activities?

Prerequisites

What do students need to know before this session?

Resources to be used by student

What resources will be used? Will you tell students which resources to use or will they select their own?

14.2 *Continued*

Evaluation

How will you evaluate learning? Will this be ongoing throughout the session or presented at the end in the form of a test or quiz? How will you record evidence of achievement?

Session plan and timetable

What will you cover in each phase of the session? E.g. introduction, development, consolidation, closing.

Resources required to deliver the session

✓ BEST FOR

- guiding the planning process
- providing a useful resource for yourself and other colleagues to use when developing and delivering the session
- those new to teaching or developing new material
- providing a reference when reviewing what has not worked in an existing session.

✚ MORE

- Enhance your lesson plan and timetable with detailed notes for yourself on running the session. This may include reminders of key points for introducing and summarizing activities. Add in another column (or section) for your post-session reflections.
- Use a pro forma to structure your lesson planning (such as example **14.2**). This will help ensure nothing is forgotten in the planning process and will also enable you to tie assessment to outcomes.

❗ WATCH OUT

- Be careful when using 'off the shelf' lesson plans, as you will need to review them in order to judge suitability for your learners and your circumstances.

➜ FURTHER READING

JISC Netskills (n.d.) *Teaching Information skills: materials for secondary schools*, www.netskills.ac.uk/content/projects/eduserv-info-lit/infoskills-materials.html.

LibraryInstruction.com, http://www.libraryinstruction.com/lessons.html.

SOS for Information Literacy, http://www.informationliteracy.org/.

Teaching Resources from the BBC, http://www.bbc.co.uk/schools/teachers/.

15 Storyboards

A storyboard is a visual planning method most often used in film and television, involving taking snapshots of a story and displaying them in a static diagram. The storyboard is usually annotated to explain what has happened between one frame and the next. Storyboards are a helpful planning tool for writing and designing learning.

Once you have decided your aims and learning outcomes, brainstorm the possible activities you could use to achieve those aims. They may include lectures, demonstrations, discussions, practical activities and handout material. Break your material down into blocks that can form the frames of the storyboard. You may wish to write each frame on a separate card or sticky note so the order can be easily rearranged. For each activity or block, make notes on the purpose of the activity, the learning outcome it contributes to, the learning style it engages, how active the learner is, and so on.

An example of a storyboard used for planning teaching sessions is shown in example **15.1** and a sample template created by Connie Malamed and used to plan e-learning resources such as videos and screencasts is shown in example **15.2**.

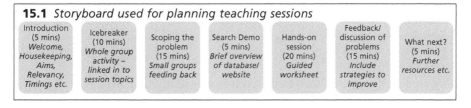

15.1 *Storyboard used for planning teaching sessions*

Sequence the blocks into a logical order and review how they fit. Ensure the activities flow and build on each other. A common sequence is to follow Kolb's (1984) experiential learning cycle: having the experience, reviewing/reflecting on the experience, concluding/learning from the experience and planning/trying out what you have learned.

15.2 *Source: http://thelearningcoach.com/elearning_design/storyboards-for-elearning/, Reproduced with permission.*

Module and Lesson Name (See example of a storyboard on next page.)	Screen number (unique identifier)
Visual description or sketch goes here.	Narration or script goes here.
Interactions, branching and programming notes go here.	Misc Notes can go here

Giving Cats Medicine: Psyching Yourself for the Job	M1L2S4 (module 1, lesson 2, screen 4)
How do you really feel? ☐ I am looking forward to placing a pill down my cat's throat. ☐ I'd rather have a root canal. ☐ I plan to hire a cat consultant to do this three times a day. ☐ I know my cat will outsmart me, so it's hopeless. ☐ My cat has very long claws. How do you think I feel?	Narration: Prior to attempting to administer a pill to a cat, it is important to achieve the correct frame of mind. In order to do this, you must face your true feelings about the experience. Select all the items that express your feelings.
If user clicks 1, go to screen 5. If user clicks 2, 4, 6, go to screen 6. If user clicks 3, go to screen 7.	Notes: Female narrator projecting a soothing voice.

✓ BEST FOR

- planning sessions
- designing learner materials
- using as a learning activity, e.g. with groups in the visual arts and younger students.

+ MORE

- Storyboarding can also be used with students in lieu of describing information verbally or on a flip chart. Identifying, finding, evaluating and using information contains a narrative thread and this can be turned into a storyboard.
- Combine this with the poster tour concept (see **Poster tours**). Each group is asked to provide one frame – dealing with identifying or finding information, for example. Each frame is put up and the different groups asked to comment, add to or otherwise amend the frames as they move around the room. The final set of amended frames becomes the complete storyboard and can be the subject of a class discussion or even, if time allows, a production.
- Ask learners to create a script rather than a storyboard or to create a complete visual representation of their search for information.

⁝ WATCH OUT

- When using storyboards as a learning activity with students, ensure that all learners are involved in the process by allocating clear tasks. You should also be very clear in the objectives of the process and in setting goals. This will be an unusual process for many learners and they may need more time to understand and conceptualize exactly what you want them to do.
- When using storyboards for planning, don't let the storyboard become an end in itself and avoid devoting a disproportionate amount of time to its development.

⋙ REFERENCE

Kolb, D. (1984) *Experiential Learning*, Prentice Hall.

Acknowledgement

Many thanks to Connie Malamed at http://the learningcoach.com for permission to reproduce her storyboard.

Delivery

16 Body language

Remember that each teaching session that you run, especially if it is in front of a large group, is a performance. Everyone has a different performing style, and you should not try to be someone that you are not, but regardless of your personal style you will need to find a way to keep the learners' attention and interest. You may be expected to deliver several sessions in a day (for example, inductions), and it is important to recognize that although you may be tired and bored with the session it will be a unique experience for the learner. They will not want or expect to see someone who is clearly bored with repeating both process and content.

Body language is key to maintaining the performance. There are many good books and sites on body language and this tip can only briefly mention some of the key aspects, but at least:

- Make eye contact with people in the room, especially when answering questions. You could choose a few people at random and switch your eye contact between them during the session. This can help to make the session seem more personal to you and ease any nerves that come with working with a large group.
- Face the audience – do not turn your back and speak to a flip chart or screen.
- Try not to move around too much but also try not to stand too still.
- Try not to fiddle with pencils, rings or any other props.
- Maintain a friendly and approachable demeanour, remembering to smile and sound enthusiastic about your topic.
- Avoid folding your arms and holding your hands near your face – this may come across as 'closed', and also will make it harder for people to hear what you are saying. Similarly, if you are sitting down, have an open body shape – try not to cross your arms and legs.

✓ BEST FOR

- any presenting situation.

✚ MORE

- Ask someone that you trust to be honest to observe you with the specific aim of commenting on your body language. This can be daunting but it could be very useful at picking up traits of which you were previously unaware.
- Alternatively, take a video of yourself and note any mannerisms you have – it is often uncomfortable viewing but can really help highlight your habits!

⁙ WATCH OUT

- Don't let the 'rules' of body language dominate your performance. Thinking about your stance, or whether you are moving too little or too much, will inevitably detract from the running of the session.
- Watch out for the body language of your learners too – it can help you judge how your session is going. It is well worth learning more about body language to help you communicate more effectively with your learners. However, there are no hard and fast rules – you may think that someone who yawns is bored, but they may have just had a late night! Sometimes what seems like a frowning face may actually be a person in deep concentration who is interested in everything you are saying.

➜ FURTHER READING

Bradbury, A. (2006) *Successful Presentation Skills,* 3rd edn, Kogan Page.

Wharton, T. (2009) *Pragmatics and Non-verbal Communication,* Cambridge University Press.

17 Collaboration

Teaching is rarely a simple interaction between teacher and learner. The learning environment will have been shaped by a number of other people – other teachers, academics, IT specialists, technicians, friends and family – and physical factors, such as buildings, equipment, learning resources, and so on. You need to take these into consideration and work with the other participants in the process to enhance the learning experience.

This is especially the case when you are working within an organization. This may be within education (school, college, university or community education), law, a health service or in a corporate environment.

There are many different elements to collaboration. For example:

- Liaising with others to understand what the learner is expected to do with the information he or she will learn how to access. Your contacts might be teaching staff or faculty in education or staff developers in corporate and commercial environments.
- Working with IT and other technical staff to match your teaching to the real environment that the learner will face. It can be especially off-putting if you base your induction sessions on using systems in a desktop environment that your learners will never use. Also be aware of how passwords will work away from your training room.
- Talking to learners to find out the learning context (how much time do they have, access to equipment, etc.).

An effective way to start to look at the barriers to collaboration is this staff development activity, on 'Building a teaching team' (discussed in Webb and Powis, 2004). First of all, draw up a grid with the major stakeholders in supporting learning or delivering training. An example (17.1) relevant to university education is given – you can add or rename columns as you wish.

Ask participants to come up with one or two words to describe each category from the perspective of the others. For example, librarians might state that academics are arrogant and that students see them as bossy. This

17.1			
Librarian	Academic	Students	IT technicians
Librarian			
Academic			
Student			
IT technician			

exposes prejudices and brings home what preconceptions you bring into any negotiation or interaction with those groups. Once you are aware of your biases, it is easier to focus on shared goals.

✓ BEST FOR

- all teaching and staff development.

✚ MORE

- Replace the grid with a simple brainstorming activity.

❢ WATCH OUT

- Do not make assumptions about people or circumstances – if you are working with colleagues from other countries this can be particularly risky, as the status and qualifications of different kinds of staff and the relative status of students will vary.
- Do not bring your prejudices about others into the exercise: it is important to remain neutral.

❖ REFERENCE

Webb, J. and Powis, C. (2004) *Teaching Information Skills: theory and practice*, Facet Publishing.

18 Computer labs

Computer labs are often the preferred environments for information skills sessions. They give the opportunity for hands-on learning but they are also often the only teaching room available. This can cause problems, as they are not the most flexible of spaces.

Firstly, if you are in a computer lab then use the computers! This may seem obvious but there is a temptation to lecture for longer than is needed or warranted. If learners are sat in front of a screen then they will expect to be using it.

Lay down ground rules early on. It is worth reminding learners to give their full attention during presentations rather than using a computer – it is courteous to you as a teacher but also to fellow learners. (It is interesting to note, however, that many presenters now encourage interaction with learners through a tool such as Twitter, which means that learners will be typing throughout a presentation!)

✓ BEST FOR

- interactive work
- providing practical experience.

✚ MORE

- If you are using a projector or Smart Board, ensure it can be seen clearly from all areas of the lab. If the layout allows, encourage learners to move in order to see better – sometimes they feel the need to sit next to their computer even when they are not using it.
- Try using a hand-held device to forward slides during presentations. Many computer labs have an awkward layout and the presenter's machine may be tucked into a corner – a hand-held mouse or pointer will free you to move to a better position to engage with learners.
- For groups who cannot resist using computers during presentations,

consider using software (such as NetSupport School, www.netsupportschool.com, or Net Control 2, www.netcontrol2.com) that allows you to control the machines. It is easier to follow on a PC than to look at a big screen in many computer labs. However, note that your learners will probably not be looking at you during the presentation. This can also be useful in large or awkward labs where seeing a presentation screen may be difficult.

- The same software can usually allow students to display what they are finding onto all screens or a display screen. This can be a powerful way of rewarding and reinforcing good practice and involving the whole group.
- Try to allow for joint working at a PC. Peer learning is a powerful tool, especially when you have differing levels of ability or experience in a class.
- Try to team teach or use a teaching assistant to help with inevitable password problems.
- If software fails or computers go down, then do not try to muddle through. If using the computers is essential to the achievement of the learning objectives then cancel or postpone the session until they are available.
- Make sure you regularly check how learners are getting on, but don't peer too long over their shoulders. Simply asking how a learner is doing will often elicit a question which a learner may have been reluctant to ask.
- Do not take over when helping a learner – if you really need to take the mouse to demonstrate something, always ask first.
- The computer lab idea can be made into a more flexible environment by using laptops instead of fixed PCs.

⁝ WATCH OUT

- As already mentioned, be careful that learners do not immediately log on and go to social networking sites or start surfing the web. Control software can help here but set clear ground rules and move around the lab, if possible, to discourage this behaviour.
- Computer rooms are notorious for often being too hot – make sure you are prepared for this by checking you know how to adjust the air conditioning or open windows. If you teach in a variety of environments it is a good idea to wear clothing in layers so you can be prepared for varying room temperatures.

19 Cultural relevance

We all have cultural biases based on our experiences, age, background and so on. This is different from prejudice, which should have no place in teaching, but it can make engaging with learners difficult if we are unaware of the differing cultural backgrounds and reference points.

Cultural bias in teaching is most obviously manifested in the way that you expect learners to interact with you and with each other, and in the examples that you use to illustrate your teaching. For example, for learners from some cultures, the democratic environment of some British university classes (where teachers might expect to be addressed by their first names), can be very disconcerting.

Although you should design teaching sessions that will facilitate the achievement of your learning outcomes, it is worth considering whether certain activities are appropriate for your learners. For example, it may be unrealistic in the UK to expect international female Muslim students to be enthusiastic participants in group work alongside British male students. Likewise, peer pressure on some British male groups may make them act as cynics and seem to be disengaged – remember there has always been a strong anti-intellectual streak, especially in England – so expecting effective collaborative brainstorming may cause problems for you.

Personal cultural biases can be reflected in the examples used in teaching. Be careful not to use too many references to alcohol if you are teaching students from teetotal religions or cultures, or refer to TV programmes or music that make you seem hopelessly out of date. A self-deprecating tone may get you through but it is better to stick to mainstream references that everyone can understand.

This is really about knowing your students. Make an effort to find out about your groups before you see them and be sensitive towards them. Make an effort to check your own references too – sensitive peer observation can help here.

✓ BEST FOR

- all teaching.

✚ MORE

- Don't let your concerns stifle you – you should not be worried about political correctness. Just be aware of the effect on your learners of what you do and say.

❗ WATCH OUT

- If you make a faux pas then simply apologize and move on – you can reflect later.

20 Demonstrations

Demonstrations are a core part of many teaching and training sessions. Many information skills demonstrations involve 'live' searching using an internet source, be it a search engine or subscription database. Live demonstrations are useful to familiarize learners with a database prior to hands-on practical sessions, or to add a dynamic element to a presentation. Any demonstration requires practice and preparation to be successful, but you must also be prepared for the unexpected as things can often go wrong!

✓ BEST FOR

- familiarizing learners with a task before practical sessions
- highlighting tips, tricks and pitfalls
- providing practical experience 'by proxy' if there is no time for a hands-on session.

+ MORE

- Tailor your demonstration to your audience to ensure it is relevant.
- Practise so you are confident in what you plan to demonstrate.
- Take screen-shots of key features in case you have a problem with your internet connection (or if you are producing step-by-step handouts).
- Do not rush.
- If you have to type search terms as part of your demonstration, consider having them ready prepared and copied to the clipboard – simply paste into the search box when you need to. This saves you problems with mistyping.
- Alternatively, bookmark a search results page – this means the search can be run without you having to type in your search terms.
- Create a screencast of a demonstration using a tool such as Screenr (www.screenr.com/) or Jing (www.techsmith.com/jing). This records your online activity as well as giving you the option of providing narration.

This could be used instead of a live demonstration or as a backup if needed. After the session, screencasts could be placed on a website for further reference.

- Ask for examples from the class.

❢ WATCH OUT

- Do not be tempted to demonstrate too many features. Just select the most useful or those which may need more explanation.
- Remember to check your demonstrations just before your session to make sure everything works, especially if you are using an unfamiliar training room. This can be especially important if you are using a different software environment or browser.

21 Discipline

Information professionals are often beset by doubts about whether they are really teachers, this sometimes leading to an unwillingness to exercise the necessary authority and control in the classroom.

Discipline does not mean a bullying, dominant personality cowing learners into silence. It means setting ground rules early in your relationship with the learners and then following these rules consistently. It is for you to set the rules, but they may include:

- **Lateness**. You may want to go to the extreme of locking the door a set time after the start of your session or you may be more liberal – but do set and maintain expectations.
- **Noise**. You should not be tolerant of people chatting over you. Some teachers will simply raise their voice over the chatting group but this will rarely do anything other than make you look weak. Either fall into silence yourself or confront the group directly. This applies to other forms of disruptive behaviour like making calls on a phone or generally messing about rather than working on the tasks that you have set.

Do not be afraid to confront bad behaviour. If possible, try to deal with a disruptive person individually rather than causing a confrontation in front of a group. There may be a cause for that behaviour which can be addressed. However, do not be afraid to ask people to leave the class if warnings are ignored and disruptive behaviour persists (although with children this may be difficult). As a teacher you should control the teaching environment. You will almost certainly find that the majority of your group is as offended by disruptive behaviour as you are and that you will be thanked for confronting it. See **Dominant participants** for further tips on how to deal with difficult learners.

✓ BEST FOR

- groups.

✚ MORE

- Be careful not to make the problem worse. If something is irritating you but not disrupting the class as a whole (texting, for example), confronting the problem will actually be a more disruptive act than the original one. Choose your interventions to minimize disruption rather than escalate it.

❗ WATCH OUT

- Never lose control of yourself. Try to stay calm and measured in the face of ill manners or bad behaviour. By escalating the situation you will only disrupt the learning more than it has been already.

→ FURTHER READING

Race, P. and Pickford, R. (2007) *Making Teaching Work: 'teaching smarter' in post-compulsory education*, Sage, 81–94.

22 Dominant participants

Dominant participants can disrupt your teaching session, both in terms of taking your attention away from other learners and throwing your timetable into disarray. There are different types of dominant participants, including the know-it-all, the talker and the deliberately disruptive learner who does not want to be there. It should be noted that a dominant participant is not necessarily being deliberately difficult: some may be naturally talkative and others actually may be trying to help you by contributing their thoughts and knowledge. They may be unaware of the impact their behaviour is having on the rest of the group. Of course, the wider group dynamic plays a part – it might be that one participant becomes dominant because the rest of the learners are so passive, and a slightly different mix of individuals would create a really lively group with several engaged, talkative learners.

The first tip for dealing with dominant participants is simply to monitor how your group of learners is interacting and identify if there are any group dynamics which are a cause for concern. Thinking about your learners as individuals as well as a group is an important part of effective teaching, and you must be just as conscious of this as you are of the content you intend to cover.

✓ BEST FOR

- ensuring you do not get distracted by focusing on one individual.

+ MORE

- If someone asks questions during a presentation which take you off-track, simply state you are happy to discuss this further with them after the presentation, but currently you need to move on.
- If you really want to avoid disruptions during presentations, ask for any questions and comments to be raised at the end.
- During group activities you will need to observe the contributions from

each participant. If you find someone is dominating, gently interrupt and ask for the opinions and thoughts of other group members.

- Try to build in methods of encouraging group participation, for example, giving out sticky notes to each person for them to write their own thoughts and ideas on. Ask for these to be stuck to a flip chart. This can then be used as a basis for discussion.

- Rather than ask for volunteers for activities (for example, giving feedback from a group activity), assign tasks yourself. Be careful, however, as you may take some people out of their comfort zone which may be difficult for some learners. Alternatively, you could just say you want a different person to do each task, thereby preventing the same person volunteering every time.

- Dominant participants are not only evident in face-to-face classes: they can be just as overwhelming in online learning environments. Find ways of structuring participation so that those who try to dominate others are made to be quiet for a while – this might be done by limiting the number of posts that can be made in a set time.

- You may also find that setting group work is a way of reducing the impact of one individual, as he or she can only speak to a smaller section of your learners. Equally, it may be that an activity draws out your other participants and they start to gain in confidence and increase their contribution to the learning and teaching event.

✵ WATCH OUT

- Following the strategies above will help you cope with a dominant participant, but do not let them disrupt your session to the detriment of others. If you feel someone is being deliberately difficult, have a quiet word and ask if there is anything you can do to address their issues with the session. If not, do not be afraid to ask them to leave.

→ FURTHER READING

Race, P. and Pickford, R. (2007) *Making Teaching Work: 'teaching smarter' in post-compulsory education*, Sage, 81–94.

23 Feedback to learners

Giving feedback on your learners' performance or development is a fundamental part of the teaching process. All learners need to know how they are progressing, even if all you do is provide a few positive comments in a workshop or a suggestion that they try a different way of approaching a problem.

You will need to provide formal feedback for summative assessment, but you should always make some attempt to give developmental and positive feedback on how learners are achieving the learning outcomes.

Feedback need not be done formally (it is always associated with the comments sheet attached to the returned piece of work or the scrawled comments on the essay), but you should follow some fundamental principles:

- Publish the learning outcomes – this is good practice, anyway. Tell the learners what they will be able to do at the end of the learning event, and the assessment criteria (if it is a piece of formal assessment) and give feedback based on them. For example, if you say that at the end of the workshop your learners will be able to find and evaluate sources on something, then your feedback should be about how far they have achieved that.
- Be specific, and tell the learners exactly what they have done well (so they can replicate it) or what they need to do to improve. 'Well done' is nice to hear, but: 'Well done, your keywords for that search were very good' identifies what they were doing right.
- Include ways to improve. All feedback should ideally be developmental, so if something has not gone quite right then provide your comments in terms that will help the learner to improve. 'You'll need better keywords next time' should really be: 'Think about ways that that concept could be expressed differently'. You should give illustrative examples.
- Encourage peer support. In most groups there will be different levels of ability and understanding. Some of the most effective feedback comes from friends and colleagues as they help one another, particularly during

practical tasks. Encourage this by setting up pair or small group work.

- Encourage critical reflection. Give learners time to digest and process your comments. This can be by setting up another task to reinforce the learning encouraged by your feedback or it could be by following up immediate comments later, perhaps by e-mail or through a virtual learning environment.

✓ BEST FOR

- all occasions.

✚ MORE

- As well as verbal or written feedback, think about using audio files or Web 2.0 technology to provide a different approach – see the separate tips on **Audio feedback**, **Blogs** and **Wikis**.
- Feedback on learning can be a two-way process, and you can develop the learning opportunity further by encouraging the learner to engage in reflection and discussion on his or her performance. You can open a dialogue in a number of ways. For example, you could ask your learners to assess their own learning (see **Self-assessment**) – in summative assessment you ask them to assign a mark to a piece of work and then compare their assessment with yours. This provides an opportunity to provide feedback not only on the learning, but also on their assessment of it. A simpler approach might be just to ask the learners to provide some kind of reflective commentary on what they have learnt and how they might change or develop their practice on the basis of the knowledge, skills and experience they have acquired.
- Alternatively you could start a discussion at the end of a session (this can be face-to-face or online), asking learners about how they think they have done, what they felt were the key learning points and what they will change about their practice in the future.

❢ WATCH OUT

- If you are giving a mark then the learners may only be interested in getting that and not listening to any feedback. An audio file can help with this as you can leave the mark until the end.

→ FURTHER READING

Askew, S. (2000) *Feedback for Learning*. RoutledgeFalmer.

Irons, A. (2008) *Enhancing Learning Through Formative Assessment and Feedback*, Routledge.

24 Handouts

Some documentation would usually be given to back up a teaching session; indeed most learners would expect it (even if they never referred to it again). Handouts can function as a security blanket for teacher and learner alike, and that is a useful function as long as they do not dominate your preparation. Perhaps the most useful function that they perform is that of allowing you to teach in generalities, knowing that the detail is included in the handout. So, for example, if you are looking at information sources in a particular subject or for a particular function, you can list them in a handout whilst concentrating in the session on the broader aspects of information retrieval – keywords, search construction, and so on.

Do not let the distribution of handouts interfere with your session. If possible, have them on the seats, on a table near to the entrance or sent out beforehand. If you need to give them out during the session either ask a learner to do it or put some at the end of each row or line of students. Introduce them: 'On your chair you will find' or: 'The handout contains all you need to know, so don't worry about making notes'.

Remember that handouts take time to write well and cost money and time to produce, so make them relevant and useful. Take care in their production – they should look professional and have correct spelling and grammar. They will reflect the professionalism of the person who hands them out so be careful when using handouts produced by others. It might be tempting to recycle but there are dangers in this: are you sure that they are relevant to your teaching, for example? This applies to your handouts too – reappraise their usefulness and currency every time that you use them.

✓ BEST FOR

- all sessions – they will reinforce and add to your input during the session
- learners with additional needs – handouts can be especially helpful to reinforce the learning activities.

+ MORE

- You may want to use partially completed handouts to aid concentration within the group. Text with words or phrases missing that learners can add to as you speak may be useful to encourage more active listening and note-taking.
- Create a more dynamic handout using the web – allow interaction and questioning using social software. For example, a blog post could be used for supporting material meaning learners could post questions via the comments option. However, this does have the disadvantage that the learner may not look at the material after the session.

? WATCH OUT

- Always make sure that you give something above that which is included in the handout during your session – the learner must get some added value from your input or they might as well simply read the handout!
- Think carefully about the usability and legibility of your handouts. Would learners who are dyslexic or visually impaired be able to derive full benefit from them? Using pastel paper and sans serif fonts (minimum font size twelve) should enhance the legibility. The same consideration should apply if you are providing copies of PowerPoint slides: it can be useful to have some copies of the slides in the half-size 'two-up' format (two slides per page) for learners who might struggle to see the smaller font sizes. This may not just be people who are dyslexic but also older learners who do not like using varifocals, or even learners who might use your slides as the basis for mind maps.
- If possible, try to find out in advance if any of your learners will require a specific format of handout.

25 Inclusion

It is good practice to consider the needs of your learners and ensure no one is disadvantaged or alienated by the methods you use. There is also a legal requirement to ensure your teaching is accessible to disabled learners. This may at first seem daunting, but often this can be achieved by just following some simple steps. You should also find that by taking into account different needs, you have improved the learning experience for everyone.

If possible, find out in advance if any learners have any specific needs, such as physical access to the training room, any requirement for assistive technology or audio or visual aids, or if any support workers will be present. Materials may require distribution in alternative formats or printing out in a larger or different font.

It is difficult to create a teaching experience that is right for everyone, as sometimes you may find needs conflict (for example, you may require bright lighting on your presentation so you can be lip-read, but the bright lighting may affect someone else who is light-sensitive – this situation happened to one of the present authors!). You should do your best to ensure you have addressed any additional requirements, but it is also up to your learners to alert you to their needs.

Inclusive practice is not just about disability, but rather about assuring access for all learners. **Cultural relevance** is discussed in a separate tip, but it is also important to consider the impact of gender on learning and teaching.

Being aware that gender can play a role in learning is important to the design and delivery of your teaching. It is not the place of this book to enter the debate on whether boys or girls are disadvantaged through educational systems, but it is clear that the gender mix of a group will affect what works within a session. Think about gender when you are forming groups and try to establish a workable compromise – there are dangers for participation in having a gender imbalance.

✓ BEST FOR

- This underpins all our learning and teaching practice.

✚ MORE

- Ask on a booking form for any additional needs such as access or dietary requirements.
- Try to provide an opportunity for learners to raise any issues during your teaching and aim to be flexible in order to address the needs if you can.
- When writing materials ensure you take steps to meet current accessibility guidance and plan designs with clarity in mind (e.g. fonts, colours and use of language).
- Be careful with your body language – try not to hold anything (your hand, a cup) near your mouth or turn away from the audience as people may be lip-reading.
- Think carefully about the words that you use: avoid using slang and make your sentences short and clear.

❗ WATCH OUT

- Remember it is usually a legal requirement to anticipate and proactively make adjustments for disabled learners; do not be caught out by an accessibility issue in your teaching. Ensure you are familiar with the law in your country.

→ FURTHER READING

UK-based JISC Techdis (www.techdis.ac.uk) has a wide range of resources relating to inclusion and accessibility. Their JISC Techdis Staff Training packs include a resource called 'Designing Effective Training Workshops', which focuses on producing an inclusive and effective workshop. It can be downloaded at: www.jisctechdis.ac.uk/techdis/resources/detail/investinyou/DesigningWorkshops.

26 Interruptions

Interruptions can and will occur during your teaching career. How you handle them is really down to your personality and the situation but you must address them. The worst thing that you can do is to ignore them. Do not let them overwhelm you (or your memories of running learning and teaching events), but do try to manage them.

Common sources of interruption:

- **Dominant personalities**. Try to avoid eye contact that might provoke a question or comment, ask others for their comments, or suggest that you meet at the end of the session to talk through the issues being raised. See the tip on **Dominant participants** for an extended discussion of this issue.
- **Mobile phones and other electronic interruptions**. Set clear expectations about these at the start of the session (remember that some people may need to be contactable during sessions for work, childcare or other personal reasons). If an interruption, such as a phone call, does happen then it is better not to ignore it – the learners' attention will have already moved to the distraction. Isolate the event by asking the person to leave the group if they do take the call. Do not humiliate a learner if he or she has simply forgotten to turn off a phone but wait patiently while they deal with it. If you are working with learners who are very likely to be contacted – for example, a workshop with healthcare professionals who may be on call – explain at the beginning of the class where they can take a call without causing disruption.
- **External noise**. If the noise is so bad that you cannot be heard properly or is so distracting that it is clearly affecting the learning environment then do not be afraid to stop the session. If you can ask the noise-makers to stop with some chance of success then you should do so, but if it is unavoidable then stop the session and try to rearrange. Struggling through will probably achieve little – you must be in control of the environment as much as possible.

- **Latecomers**. Ignore them. Making an issue of the lateness at the time will only exacerbate the interruption. Do try to have a word with the latecomers at some point though, stressing how disruptive lateness is. There is an extended discussion on this topic in the tip on **Latecomers**.

✓ BEST FOR

- all learning and teaching events.

✚ MORE

- If possible, mitigate the chances of interruption by setting clear ground rules for your learners, by scouting the environment you have to work in beforehand and by liaison with those who arrange the teaching. If these things are not possible then you may want to have some exercises or activities that you can fit into the session to cope with noise or disruption.

⁝ WATCH OUT

- Dealing with the interruption can sometimes be more disruptive than the interruption itself. Be sure that your intervention will improve the situation – an example is intervening to stop someone texting. This may be irritating to you but most other learners will not have noticed it so your intervention will actually be the interruption to their learning. And remember, in Twitter-conscious times, participants may be Tweeting about the session!

27 Jokes and humour

Humour can provide a way of engaging learners by catching their attention and making the session enjoyable. Incorporating jokes into your session, however, can be more problematic, the simple rule being: do not tell jokes unless you are a comedian. If you do decide to joke, remember a few rules:

- Timing is all – there are times to tell jokes and times when you should not. Your comic timing is also crucial and this is something that is very difficult to learn.
- Never use sarcasm to get a laugh when you are in a position of power – it will be destructive to your relationship with the group and especially the individual the comment was aimed at.
- If you must joke then make it relevant to the situation – rambling tales about what happened to you on the way to the classroom will only deflect from the learning.

But do use humour – gentle humour, especially self-deprecating, will show a human and accessible side to you and ease the learning process.

✓ BEST FOR

- all sessions.

✚ MORE

- Change your jokes – a tired joke will almost certainly be an unfunny one.
- Consider using a light-hearted story to introduce humour into your sessions – see **Storytelling** for more details.

❗ WATCH OUT

- If no one laughs then stop joking!

- Ensure your jokes will not offend – consider the backgrounds of your learners. (See **Cultural relevance**.)

28 Latecomers

Latecomers are an inevitable part of the teaching experience. Some teachers lock the doors after five or ten minutes but this is not always possible or desirable.

A group arriving late means that you will have to reappraise your plans. Always build in some activities that you can leave out if disaster strikes, preferably backing them up with handouts or online resources. Never try to continue and cram in everything that you originally planned to do if you don't now have the time.

Individual latecomers can be as disruptive as you let them be. Have handouts near to the door or on spare chairs so that they can pick them up when they arrive. Try not to acknowledge them more than common courtesy (a smile if they apologize, etc.). Pause in speaking if they are disrupting the group in finding a place but do not be tempted to make sarcastic comments. It may be more embarrassing for them than it is annoying for you, and is certainly irritating for those participants who have arrived on time.

If an individual joins your class after group work or practical work has started then quickly brief them before letting them join in. This should mitigate any disruption to the group that they are joining. But remember, if they arrive too late, you could refuse entry. Don't forget that the latecomer's colleagues are the most disadvantaged by this kind of behaviour.

✓ BEST FOR

- This is probably most often an issue in post-compulsory education, i.e. in colleges and universities, but will also happen in the workplace.

✚ MORE

- The latecomer may try to speak to you as they arrive, asking about handouts, what has been covered so far, and so on. Always deflect this by saying that you will see them later. Engaging latecomers in conversation will only make the disruption worse.

❣ WATCH OUT

You need to understand why you have latecomers. There are three possible reasons:

- Your learner(s) were unavoidably detained in another class or appointment. If this happens, often the majority of your class will be late and you will need to reassess what you were planning to cover.
- An individual was unavoidably detained – for a legitimate reason.
- One or more individuals just could not be bothered to turn up on time. This is an issue of classroom discipline and the respect that those learners have for their peers and the learning experience.

If you apply sanctions (locking the door after ten minutes or refusing to add latecomers' names to a classroom register) then do make them clear in advance. It may be helpful to find out if there are organizational (or local) policies about how to handle latecomers.

29 Managing groups

Activities can succeed or fail depending on the groups you create. It is often very effective to break a larger group into smaller, more manageable groups for practical work. They can work in a more focused way, there is often plenty of opportunity for active learning and discussion and it is more efficient of the teacher's time, especially in terms of giving feedback and support. Getting the right mix of learners in each group is easy if you use some simple techniques.

Try to create your groups sensitively: take into account gender, cultural differences, ability and even age and status. For example, if you are running a staff development session with a mixture of senior and junior staff or people with a mixture of professional backgrounds (think a mixture of health professionals or library and IT staff), consider whether mixing up the levels and occupations will help or hinder the achievement of your learning objectives. You can, of course, simply allow learners to form their own groups but this risks having groups who form their own agendas and who may just engage in social loafing.

You should give a justification for dividing learners into groups. Participants will want to know what the benefits are of working in a group on that activity and what they will gain from group work that will be more effective than working individually. This is critical: remember that learners will only really engage if they can see some value – if they can see what will be learnt by that engagement and that they will not be disadvantaged in terms of their own achievements by working with others.

Keep the work focused and time-bound. If you are expecting feedback then it is wise to warn the groups beforehand and ask them to nominate someone to act as rapporteur or leader.

Always try to circulate around the learning space unobtrusively while the groups are working; you can give valuable feedback by doing this and keep groups on track with the task. It will also allow you to gauge timings – you may need to shorten the time allowed or allow more. Try not to interrupt any discussion but sit at the edge and only comment for clarification, to reinforce a useful point or to move them gently back onto the point if they have strayed away.

✓ BEST FOR

- ensuring the right mix of learners in a group
- large groups
- practical sessions with limited resources
- encouraging peer support.

✚ MORE

- Try breaking up friendship groups by using the traffic light method (each person is allocated 'red', 'amber' or 'green'), by counting off people around to form the number of groups required, using colour-coded badges or arranging the room layout to create groups.
- Place your materials in different coloured folders and divide groups according to colour (this also means your materials are bright and attractively presented). Alternatively, use some kind of prop to divide groups – e.g. give out coloured stickers or sweets. This can act as an ice-breaker as well as helping divide groups. Groups could be allocated in this way randomly or prearranged, if you want to ensure a particular mix of learners within a group.
- Do not be afraid to change groups if they are not working. A failing group can be very disruptive in a workshop environment.
- Feeding back from a group can be daunting for some people and valuable time can be taken up in debating who the spokesperson should be. An alternative is to circulate around the groups as the session progresses and to make brief notes as you go. You can then summarize for each group and ask them to comment on your summary. A poster tour (see **Poster tours**) can be a very effective alternative.
- Group work can be enhanced by technology-enhanced learning (TEL) but you will usually need to spend longer planning the activity and may need to allow time for online discussion, interaction and resource creation. However, if you want your learners to produce a substantial outcome – such as a presentation or report – creating shared online workspaces, a wiki and a discussion forum can be very useful. For example, one of our colleagues asked groups of fine art students to

produce wiki pages on artists of their choice as a practical activity in a series of library research classes. This was very effective: participants needed to find, post and cite relevant material, and thus explored a whole range of information literacy competences (Poulton, 2010).

? WATCH OUT

- Friction or non-participation in groups are the greatest risks. Be sensitive to events and be prepared to move people if really necessary, or provide additional support to a failing group.
- Be careful about letting your learners arrange themselves into groups for this may mean you do not get a good mix of experience and opinion. Keep observing your groups for signs that they are working well together. If you find that a group is not working, try using different groups for the next task. Just divide the groups again as if that is what you had planned to do all along. No one need know the reason for the regroup!
- Always consider the number of people in your groups and whether it is appropriate for the task you have set. For example, a discussion group will struggle with only two or three participants, but if you want the group to complete a focused task in a short time then small groups will work best.

➡ REFERENCE

Poulton, A. (2010) *Fine Art Wiki: reflections on using the read/write web to develop information literacy skills in first-year fine art students*. Presentation at LILAC, Limerick, 29–31 March, unpublished.

➜ FURTHER READING

Exley, K. and Dennell, R. (2004) *Small Group Teaching: tutorials, seminars and beyond*, RoutledgeFalmer.
Macdonald, R. (1997) *Teaching and Learning in Small Groups*, SEDA.

30 Managing questions

Encouraging questions from your learners is a good way of ensuring understanding and stimulating thought. You can use questions in a variety of ways.

Support the development of an interactive questioning environment right from the start of your session. For example, you might want to ask your learners to draw up questions at the beginning of a session, using their questions to frame the event, and help define the aims and learning outcomes of the workshop. This can be particularly useful if you have learners with very specific concerns and can be an effective ice-breaker.

Alternatively, questions may be part of your dialogue with learners during a workshop, where they ask questions either individually to you during a practical or as part of a plenary session.

You need to create an atmosphere of trust and acceptance so that your learners will feel ready to ask questions, without feeling stupid. As the session leader, you will also need to use your listening skills to draw out the meaning from less than perfectly phrased questions.

✓ BEST FOR

- sessions where you are able to establish a rapport with your learners
- smaller groups, but can be adapted to work with large groups
- when you will expect groups to work together on some kind of practical activity.

✚ MORE

- When giving a presentation, state when you are happy to receive questions. Are you comfortable for learners to interrupt you or would you rather they wait until the end?
- If you take questions during a presentation, be careful not to let the question divert you from your topic. If the questioner is persistent, or the

answer will sidetrack you significantly, then simply state you will speak to that person individually afterwards.

- Another way of using questioning as an ice-breaker would be to set up a brief discussion. This could be something to provoke thought, such as 'imagining life without Google or the internet'. A quick way of gathering feedback is to ask learners to write something brief on a sticky note, which you can then collate on a wall or flip chart.
- Stop at regular intervals in your session to ask for questions.
- During practical sessions ensure you check on individuals and ask how they are getting on. Some learners may be shy about asking questions, but when approached directly they may feel more comfortable opening up to speak.

❣ WATCH OUT

- Do not let one person dominate the questioning – if this happens be polite but firm and suggest that they see or contact you after the session.

31 Managing sessions – overview

Ensuring your teaching session runs to time and that learners reach the desired learning outcome requires the ability to manage the session effectively. Starting and finishing a session are covered elsewhere in this book (see **Managing sessions – the start** and **Managing sessions – the end**): managing a session involves what goes on in-between those two points!

As a teacher you need to constantly review how your session is running and also be mindful of time passing. Moving from one activity to the next needs to be thought through – in terms of managing how the learning is delivered, as well as in terms of logistics. For example, you may be moving from one room to another. Write a lesson plan (see **Lesson planning**) to remind yourself of what you need to do, and when.

✓ BEST FOR

- Session management in both face-to-face and online environments is an essential part of effective teaching. You do not have to stand at the front with an hourglass to check your timing, but equally, you should also be conscious of the shape and structure of the session you are leading and whether or not you are on schedule.

✚ MORE

- In your introduction to the session make it clear that learners need to stick to the given timings in order to cover the required material. This need not be given in a stern way, simply ask this out of respect for other learners. Emphasize that you will be sticking to the times so if learners do not want to miss anything, they should too.
- Make sure you are clear about how much time learners have for each activity. Towards the end of the allocated time, give a five-minute warning.
- When announcing coffee or lunch breaks, give a specific time to restart the session, for example announce: 'We will be starting back at 1.45 p.m.'

rather than: 'You have forty-five minutes for lunch'. This is more definite and means times are less likely to slip. Do be conscious that if you are working with learners from a range of different countries, conceptions of time and punctuality might vary. If you think you might have stragglers, plan this into your lesson timings and allow some 'wriggle room' in the schedule so you can make up any delays.

- Do not try to give instructions for a task when people are on the move, as they will not be listening! Either give instructions *before* they move or wait until the movement has stopped.

- Observe your learners for signs of how the session is going. Does anyone look bored? Frustrated? Annoyed with another participant? Confused? You may need to intervene to get to the root of the problem. Simply by asking how things are going, you usually find the cause. You may need to think on your feet and rearrange a group or change an activity if it is not working. (See **Group work**.)

- If you find an individual is dominating the session to the detriment of others, do not be afraid to take action. (See **Dominant participants**.)

- Introduce each activity, giving clear instructions and timings. At the end of each activity ensure there is a feedback session (if appropriate) and summarize the main learning points. At the start of the next activity, recap these key points and move on.

- If you are making an essential point then it is a good idea to signpost that this is something fundamental to the understanding of the whole subject. This can be done verbally or in a handout or worksheet. There are dangers that you make everything important (why include it if it is not important?) or that learners will only choose to engage with those points that you identify. However, a well designed session will have perhaps three or four key points that need to be grasped and these will be reinforced by the rest of the input.

- Consider using 'staging' to signpost the transition between different parts of the session, i.e. signalling when you have moved on from the introduction, when assessment will take place or highlighting the concluding parts of your learning and teaching event. This involves providing some kind of sensory clue that an activity is starting or finishing. This could mean the use of a different colour slide to mark the end of presentations, the use of music, or simply a change in your body language – for example, moving to a different place in the room to indicate a change in activity. Transmitting a clear sense of structure helps the learners to shape their understanding of the learning.

❗ WATCH OUT

- If you need to intervene, resist the temptation to take over the rest of the session.
- Do not be too rigid about sticking to your timetable. Sometimes the needs of your learners may mean you need to be flexible and change your plans. You will need to make a judgement about how far to veer away from your original plans, but most of the time, changing direction in response to the session will not be noticeable to the learners and will have a much more positive outcome overall.
- Both action learning and problem-based learning are much less structured approaches in terms of signposting, as they are fundamentally learner-, rather than tutor-led. As the tips on these approaches indicate, there are still clear learning outcomes but the more experiential and unstructured the approach, the longer it takes to work effectively.

→ FURTHER READING

Race, P. and Pickford, R. (2007) *Making Teaching Work: 'teaching smarter' in post-compulsory education*, Sage.

32 Managing sessions – the start

How you start a teaching or training session has a huge effect on the engagement and expectations of your learners. You can set the tone (for example, creating an informal, friendly atmosphere), and your behaviour can ensure that you are taken seriously as someone who behaves professionally and has expert knowledge.

Ensure you give an overview of the content of the session and outline the aims and learning outcomes. This will help manage the learners' expectations. This does not need to be in detail and you can always keep a few surprises. However, letting the learners know that there will be an assessment at some point or that they will have some group work means that they are more likely to engage with your plans. There are many other ways of getting off to a good start in your session – see the tips below.

✓ BEST FOR

- motivating learners
- managing expectations
- creating the atmosphere you need.

✚ MORE

- Prepare the teaching room in advance so you are ready to welcome learners as soon as they arrive.
- Be friendly. Welcoming small talk at the start of a session can help relax learners and hopefully warm them to you.
- When formally introducing the session, ensure learners are aware of any housekeeping issues such as fire procedures, location of fire exits and availability of refreshments.
- Letting learners know what will happen also allows learners to ask questions and to let you know if they have already covered what you intended to include.

- Be enthusiastic about your topic – if you can't sound interested then why should your learners be?
- Give a timetable for the day.
- Try to include something in your introduction that emphasizes the relevance of the session. Why is it important? Why do the learners need to be there? Many learners feel they already know how to use a search engine or a library – you can have a huge impact on the motivation of your learners at this stage.
- Use the INTRO technique. When starting a session, remember to include Interest Need Time Relevance Objectives. It doesn't matter in what order you mention these, just make sure you do!
- Start with something unexpected and innovative. Try music as the learners enter the room (be careful to pick something that matches the mood that you want to create, i.e. not too soporific or too boisterous).
- Instead of going straight into a lecture, ask the learners to immediately do something practical which you can then build on later in the session (an example of an activity is for the learner to find something which you can then compare with something from a more 'academic' source).

❗ WATCH OUT

- Make time for the start of a session. It can be quite easy to start too quickly – from nerves or excitement. Be aware of this and try to speak at your usual pace, right from the beginning.

⟿ REFERENCE

The INTRO technique is included in the Stonebow Group Training Certificate materials. Details of this face-to-face course are available from: www.people1sttraining.co.uk/programmes/train-the-trainer/courses/23.

33 Managing sessions – the end

Most of the focus in planning and developing a learning and teaching event goes on the beginning and middle. This tip is all about the end. Finishing (or closing) a session is the part that is most often neglected. Teachers are so pleased that the session has gone well that they can let the final stage drift away. This is particularly easy when there is a practical activity and learners complete their tasks at slightly different times, and also when you can see that your class is all packed up and ready to go somewhere else. But remember, just as a novel or an essay has a conclusion, so should a learning and teaching event.

The best way of finishing a session is by referring back to the opening aims and learning outcomes and demonstrate how they have been achieved. This should not be just a mechanical exercise, repeating the formal aims and objectives you devised at the beginning. Tell the story of the learning and teaching event to the class instead: 'Today, we have looked at how you can use x, using y in order to do z. You have found out a, b and c . . .'

A clear conclusion provides an opportunity to focus again on the learning outcomes, and the information and positive impression you want your learners to take away with them.

✓ BEST FOR

- all formal learning and teaching events.

✚ MORE

- You can also get learners to articulate a conclusion by asking them what they will remember, or what was most important for them. If you have used an interactive activity to set aims and objectives and co-developed the content with the learners, this can be an effective way of bringing the session to a close.
- If you have time, a good way of rounding up a session is to get learners

to compile 'top tips' based on your session. Depending on the length and amount of content covered, this could be five or ten tips. This helps learners reflect, but also helps you learn about what learners found most useful about your session.

- Always make sure your learners know where they can get further support, whether it is from you specifically or a library e-mail address or phone number.
- Suggest further opportunities for development that build on the session you have just finished, although be careful not to bombard learners with too much information as they leave. A handout or follow-up e-mail could be used.
- Try to say goodbye to your learners and thank them for coming – this is your last chance to make a good impression.

❣ WATCH OUT

- Always aim to finish on time. If there is a drift to the door before you have finished then ask people why this is the case and adjust your timing accordingly.

34 Marking

Marking is associated with summative assessment – the giving of a mark or grade that indicates how the piece of work has met the assessment criteria and, therefore, the learning outcomes. Giving a mark is always good for motivating learners but be prepared to be hard (but fair). Feedback is also important – look at the tips on **Audio feedback** and **Feedback to learners**.

If you are involved with assessing work, ensure that you have clear assessment criteria. That is, what are you testing and how? Indicate to the learner what it will take to achieve each grade. Your assessment criteria are clearly linked to your learning outcomes for the programme or session. You should not be marking on anything that has not been covered in your teaching or learning activities. Further tips on marking are given below.

✓ BEST FOR

- motivating learners
- providing feedback to learners on progress.

✚ MORE

- Ensure you have an idea or example of a model answer – either in your mind or written down.
- Set aside sufficient time to mark all of the pieces of work. Have breaks but do not leave too much time between pieces – consistency is best served by marking in batches.
- Go back and look at the first few pieces of marking after you have completed a reasonable number of assessments. You will probably have been too harsh or too lenient compared to later ones. Marking is usually either criterion-referenced (each piece marked only on the assessment criteria without reference to any other piece of work) or norm-referenced (checked against other pieces to achieve a 'norm' for that level). You should not mix the two systems but it is perhaps inevitable that some

norm referencing will occur.

- Make brief notes as you go so that you can construct developmental feedback – scribbling in the margins of the work can simply mean confusion for the learner as they try to decipher your comments. If you must write on the scripts then use a pencil.
- Formative assessment can still contain an element of marking: try asking your learners to give grades for group feedback – their own and their peers. This will help groups to engage with presentations rather than nervously wait their turn or switch off once it has passed.

❗ WATCH OUT

- Marking is very labour-intensive and, if done properly, can be mentally draining. Take breaks and refresh yourself – you would not want your carefully crafted work to be assessed by someone looking at their thirty-fifth continuous script!

35 Mixed abilities

If you are teaching a group of learners, you will inevitably have to address the issue of mixed abilities, as no two learners are the same. There is potential for this to disrupt your session as you may spend more time helping one person to the detriment of the others. Alternatively, some learners may get bored if the pace is too slow for them. There are several steps you can take to address a group of learners with mixed abilities.

Setting clear prerequisites will provide a benchmark for your session. Ensure that these are stated on all the publicity for your session so learners know what is expected of them.

✓ BEST FOR

- diverse groups of learners
- most teaching situations.

✛ MORE

- Recommend pre-course training to prepare learners for your session.
- For smaller groups, ask learners to introduce themselves and explain what they hope to get out of the session: this will help you to gauge a learner's knowledge and experience.
- Set a quiz or test for learners to take prior to the session to enable you to assess their ability and/or experience. It may then be possible to 'stream' learners into groups of similar abilities.
- For paired activities, pair learners of different abilities in order that one can support the other. Make sure you observe the pair working together as you may find that one person may get frustrated or the supposedly more 'knowledgeable' person may lead the other astray! If it is not working, you may need to intervene and perhaps rearrange groups for the next task.
- Prepare additional material for faster learners and hand this out when

needed. This is better than identifying those who are struggling by giving them 'easier' material to work on.

⁝ WATCH OUT

- Do not be tempted to dumb the session down to the lowest common denominator, as this will frustrate most of the group. Offer support to those who are struggling but it is better to do this outside of the session, on a one-to-one basis, than disrupt the learning of the majority.

36 Motivation

Individuals only learn if they want to. You may be lucky enough to teach highly motivated learners who are keen to learn no matter how you design your teaching, but more likely, you will need to get them motivated. Many learners may feel confident about their own information literacy and not see the need for any specialist input, so this can be an extra challenge when teaching.

Fundamentally, there are two different kinds of motivation:

- Intrinsic motivation is when the learner finds reward by doing the task well, rather than just doing what he or she has been told to do. This is often related to the level of control over circumstances that the learner feels he or she can exercise, and the level of effort that is felt to be merited. Learners with intrinsic motivation tend to believe that they can be effective in reaching their desired goals.
- Extrinsic motivation is when the learner is influenced by external factors. This might be a desire to pass one test in order to do something he or she wants to do more (like a driving test), or for reward or punishment. Competition can provide extrinsic motivation.

Lublin (2003) summarizes the characteristics of learner motivation. Highly motivated learners may be interested in the subject matter and enjoy learning for learning's sake, taking a 'deep' approach to learning, so they try hard to learn thoroughly, internalizing all the information and using practical and reflective opportunities to turn it into personal knowledge. Those learners who focus simply on the requirements of a qualification, rather than the wider subject in general, will usually take a 'surface' or perhaps a strategic approach to learning (strategic learners do not just want to pass, they want to obtain high marks and are capable of being very organized to achieve this). In the latter cases, your learners may not engage fully with the learning process and the learning may not last. Be warned though: these distinctions can sometimes be quite glib and the effectiveness of learning is not tested until assessment or sometimes after the assessment process has been completed. Strategic learners can often pick up new content very effectively and move on quickly.

Remember as well that many participants may not come to your session with a positive self-concept of themselves as learners. This can mean that they will set themselves up to fail as they do not believe they can ever achieve the learning goals, not just in your session, but in any learning opportunity. You need to be sensitive to this, and think about how you can support these learners to achieve their goals. Sometimes learners will demonstrate challenging behaviours to mask their profound lack of confidence, especially if they do not wish to lose face in front of their peers.

✓ BEST FOR

- all groups of learners.

✚ MORE

Many learners do not demonstrate very much motivation and need the teacher to provide this motivation in some way. There are many ways you can influence the motivation of your learners:

- Show enthusiasm – if you are not interested in the subject you are teaching, how can you expect your learners to be?
- Be polite and professional – learners will take you seriously.
- Treat learners as individuals and try to address their needs if possible.
- Choose relevant examples, linked to the curriculum or the needs they have expressed.
- Try to demonstrate the benefits of your session. Show how it will help them, for example, saving time or providing better quality resources.
- Make sure the introduction to your session catches the interest of your learners (see **Managing sessions – the start**).
- Demonstrate 'quick wins' (where the learner can achieve a useful and relevant learning outcome quickly and easily) if you can.
- Make your session fun and interesting by using interactive teaching techniques, problem-based learning or games.
- Use attractive materials incorporating a range of colours and images (but do not go too over the top!). Perhaps use video or music to liven up demonstrations and presentations.

! WATCH OUT

- Some learners may never appear to be interested in what you are trying to teach. Just accept that this will happen, but remember, at least they have turned up – this may mean that although they do not appear to be very motivated, in part they do want to learn, and may take more away with them than you might suspect.

•◦ REFERENCE

Lublin, J. (2003) *An Introduction to Deep, Surface and Strategic Approaches to Learning,* http://tutors.anu.edu.au/sites/default/files/documents/lublin2003.pdf.

→ FURTHER READING

Atherton J. S. (2011) *Learning and Teaching: deep and surface learning,* http://www.learningandteaching.info/learning/deepsurf.htm

37 Multisensory approaches

Multisensory approaches to developing learning and teaching events appeal to all the senses and the range of learning styles. Rather than relying on the tutor speaking and perhaps some visual input in the form of slides or a handout, you would use a much greater array of approaches, including physical activity, a wider range of aural input (using music or other recorded voices), more visual variety (using colour and images instead of just plain text) and practical hands-on activities that would require your learners to move around. By appealing to a range of potential learning styles and creating a more stimulating environment, it is suggested that multisensory approaches to teaching can be more inclusive, especially when working with neurodiverse learners (e.g. those with dyslexia or dyspraxia). It can also simply be more engaging, especially if it is unexpected. (See **Learning styles**.) After all, doing the unexpected is a good way of getting learners' attention and signalling that this will not be the boring 'library' session they may have been expecting.

You do not have to go to great extremes to create a multimedia event when starting to use multisensory approaches. A simple starting point might be to use music to set the scene as learners enter the room or to signal a change of activity. You could use it as background for an activity or as part of the activity itself. Turning a poster tour into a version of pass the parcel by playing music and asking learners to stop at the poster or station that they are closest to when the music stops can be an effective way of lightening the mood. All of these require confidence though – if you are not sure of the rationale or you feel obliged to apologize for the music then you probably should not use it. Be careful about the music too – nothing too divisive and remember what you may think is appropriate may not seem the same to a fifteen-year-old.

✓ BEST FOR

- mature groups
- young children

- groups who are expecting a passive session.

✚ MORE

- Multisensory means just that: ways of appealing to all the senses. If you find that you are enjoying using a range of media, start to explore and develop your approaches.
- Try showing a short film or a multimedia presentation as learners enter the room.
- Leave puzzles out for learners to attempt during breaks.
- Put stress toys on the tables where learners sit – this will help those kinaesthetic learners keep moving while learning and also provide some light relief.

⁝ WATCH OUT

- Think carefully about how this will be received. You need to be comfortable in using multisensory approaches or your learners will sense your lack of conviction.
- It is also important to be careful about not patronizing your learners: music as a background for activities is fine, but young adults might not like to be reminded of a children's party through use of inappropriate music or images.
- Do not let the music play too long, and watch the reactions of your group. Surprise and engagement are good – boredom and a poor reaction to Muzak mean that you are overdoing it.

38 Nerves

Almost everyone is nervous before teaching – complacency is likely to creep in if you are not, so nerves can be good. However, being too nervous can lead to rushing, stumbling, losing control or missing things. Nerves can be calmed by breathing exercises and practice, especially working on your timing. Having strategies in place to deal with interruptions or unforeseen events can help you feel more prepared, and therefore have less to be nervous about.

It is often a good idea to plan what you are wearing: if you feel that you look good, then you immediately start to feel more confident. It can be off-putting to realize that you are going to be standing in front of other people, and they will be watching you, so dress for the occasion. And remember, that means being comfortable too!

If you are nervous about speaking to a large group, then concentrate on a few people around the room and speak as if to them individually. Having more than one focus will stop you fixing a single person with an unnerving stare!

✓ BEST FOR

- session preparation.

+ MORE

- Advice on handling nerves is often contradictory. Some guides suggest that you rehearse what you say, but this can limit spontaneity and make your delivery seem dead and unresponsive to the needs to a group of learners. It is also important to remember that timing for the real thing is often different from how it ran through in rehearsal just because there is a different social dynamic in the room.
- Do have some notes or slides to help you structure your way through a talk. Although there is a discussion elsewhere on the risks of being too tied to using PowerPoint, remember that having some prompts and a clear lesson plan will make a great difference to how well prepared you feel.

! WATCH OUT

- When you are nervous it's easy to focus on what can go wrong, or what you don't want to happen – whether this is forgetting your words, blushing, or making a mistake during a demonstration. By focusing on the negative this can be self-fulfilling as your mind becomes full of negative thoughts. Instead of dwelling on what can go wrong, try thinking positive thoughts – for example, rather than thinking: 'I mustn't blush', think: 'I will speak clearly and confidently'. This will take practice, but eventually your positive thoughts will crowd out your negative ones and move your focus from the negative.

39 One-to-one teaching/coaching

Most information skills teaching will usually involve supporting individuals in their use of information resources, either as part of a group session or while supporting individuals on an ad hoc basis within the library, often at the reference or enquiry desk (or their virtual equivalents). The UK's Chartered Institute of Personnel and Development (CIPD) defines coaching as 'developing a person's skills and knowledge so that their job performance improves . . . leading to the achievement of organizational objectives' (CIPD, 2010). It usually lasts for a short period and focuses on specific skills and goals.

Coaching is seen to be a non-directive form of development, although feedback is still provided to the learner. Coaching and one-to-one teaching can take place in formal or informal learning environments, face-to-face or mediated electronically. Remember, you may not be able to resolve all the issues that the learner brings to you, so it is best to focus on priorities and identify what should be the key learning outcome from the session.

When supporting learners, you may not necessarily have the luxury of seeing them for several sessions, but nevertheless you can still use coaching skills in your one-to-one work, even within a larger class. Remember, however, that it is a skilled activity and it is important to prepare effectively and to take up some staff development opportunities to enhance your practice.

Buckley and Caple (1996) suggest a model for one-to-one training and coaching:

- preparation
- introduction
- explanation and/or demonstration
- imitation and consolidation
- application afterwards.

This provides a good structure for planning sessions and can be used as a loose model to use when providing 'on the spot' support.

One-to-one sessions with learners can be very effective as normally you will be working with motivated participants who are often able to articulate his or her immediate concerns. You can therefore focus clearly on how to resolve the issues identified.

It is important to recognize that the session should be a dialogue, not a one-way conversation: coaching approaches are focused on listening to the learner, not being tutor-led.

✓ BEST FOR

- meeting individual needs.

✚ MORE

- Try not to take over when giving a learner help. If you need to interrupt and demonstrate at any point, ask the learner if that would be OK first. It can be tempting just to take the mouse and do it yourself!
- Remember that coaching is non-directive, and so focus on trying to suggest alternative approaches rather than saying 'don't' too often.
- Take advantage of the opportunity to work one-to-one and be aware of learning styles. You can be flexible and cater to individual needs much more effectively than when you're working with a group. For example, your learner may wish to try first and ask questions after, if needed, or he or she may prefer you to explain and demonstrate first. If a learner is uncertain, it is best to take the lead and follow a loosely planned structure, such as the model suggested earlier.
- One-to-one sessions allow you to focus on the specific information needs of that individual, so ask for a real-life problem to work through. Do not think that you are necessarily spoon-feeding (or helping your learner inappropriately). For example, even if you agree on how to structure a literature search with a learner in a one-to-one session, the learner should still have to complete the search and read the material.
- Learners often want to run before they can walk, so you may have to manage expectations and check that the basics are in place. However, coaching sessions should be flexible. What seems straightforward to a library and information professional can be very complicated to a user, while your learner might be comfortable with very complex concepts.

Similarly, you may find learners actually want you to find something for them, rather than become independent. A balance must be found between your role as an expert and teaching learners to become self-sufficient.

- Practice your listening and questioning skills to ensure you communicate effectively with your learner.

‼ WATCH OUT

- Some learners can become dependent on you – coming back time after time. This is probably a signal that you are doing too much for them within the 'tutorials', so make sure that they understand the transferable nature of the skills you are giving them and do not be afraid to gradually withdraw support – asking a colleague to take over is often a good way to do this.
- One-to-one teaching is highly effective, but is resource-intensive. You may need to think how you might manage your time or access to one-to-ones to make the most effective use of your skills without being too restrictive to learners who would benefit from access.

⇢ REFERENCES

Buckley, R. and Caple, J. (1996) *One-to-one Training and Coaching Skills*, Kogan Page.

CIPD (2010) *Coaching and Mentoring*, www.cipd.co.uk/hr-resources/factsheets/coaching-mentoring.aspx.

The Thiagi Group, *Current List of Coaching Tips*, www.thiagi.com/e-mail-coach101-tips.html.

40 Peer observation

Peer observation is the process of asking a colleague to sit in on a learning and teaching event and provide structured, developmental feedback afterwards. Formal peer observation is a very powerful developmental approach to teaching and the support of learning. There are some variations to this, but common practice is for a meeting or briefing to take place before the event. The person being observed tells the observer about the session, for example, its aims and objectives, intended learning outcomes and type of learners. You can also highlight elements of teaching you want covered but the observation should not be confined solely to these. When the session takes place the observer should make notes but not become involved in activities. The observer should be unobtrusive in the learning and teaching space but able to see both teacher and participants.

After the session the observer will give feedback to you. Some organizations have special peer observation forms that help to structure and frame the discussion, but otherwise in advance of the observation identify and agree on the areas that may be covered.

The observee should be encouraged to evaluate their own teaching immediately after the session. Some observers may also be ready to provide more detailed feedback at this time. Otherwise, another time (within a day or so) for formal feedback will be agreed and feedback given then. A written report should be available. Actions should be a part of the report and ideally agreed at the meeting.

Observers should be honest and constructive in their feedback, and observees open to constructive criticism.

David Gosling (2002) has some very helpful guidelines about what he calls peer review, rather than peer observation. The following is summarized from his website, with some added discussion points. First of all, it is important to emphasize that the process must be developmental rather than judgemental. Peer observation and review are best when they are used comprehensively as part of your teaching culture and practice, and need to include values of mutual trust and respect between observer and the observed, and acknowledgement that the intended purpose is the enhancement of teaching. After all, remember that the term is *peer* observation (or review). Partners in the observation must be committed to enhancing the quality of the teaching, but the observation and review process should be a dialogue, not just feedback.

Observers should try to promote that dialogue by asking open questions that encourage reflection and review, rather than judgements. Good teaching comes in many forms, so observers also need to be ready to debate how and why particular approaches were used, even if it is not something they would do.

✓ BEST FOR

- all teaching situations, but especially for new teachers
- getting feedback when you feel something could be improved or are trying something new
- sharing good practice
- getting new ideas.

+ MORE

- Try to be observer and observee at least once a year – you learn a lot by observing others.
- Try to arrange observation of online activities too. This is especially useful when learning techniques of online moderation.
- You can also use peer observation to give feedback and encourage dialogue on enquiry work or one-to-one tutorials.

⁝ WATCH OUT

- Peer observation can be really stressful, so avoid having your line manager observe unless it is part of a formal appraisal process.
- Avoid asking someone who will not wish to offend you – the process needs to be honest, open and developmental.

⤖ REFERENCE

Gosling, D. (2002) *Models of Peer Observation of Teaching,* LTSN: Higher Education Academy, www.heacademy.ac.uk/resources/detail/resource_database/ id200_Models_of_Peer_Observation_of_Teaching.

→ FURTHER READING

Gosling, D. (2009) *Peer Review of Teaching,* www.davidgosling.net/default.asp?iId=KEMFL.

41 PowerPoint

It sometimes seems that using Microsoft PowerPoint to deliver a presentation is compulsory. PowerPoint is a sophisticated presentation tool but is often used badly, leading to the phrase 'Death by PowerPoint'. The mistake usually made is to have too much text on each slide, made worse if the speaker simply reads it out. When using PowerPoint, consider carefully *why* you are using it and make sure you focus on the needs of your learners. If you want to give your learners a detailed handout, do not be tempted to put all of the information on your slides. Instead, just use the slides to deliver the key points. It can be helpful, though, to put any technical vocabulary or difficult words on the slides to minimize the risk of misunderstanding. This is especially important if you are working with a group of learners who do not have English as a first language as your text will provide an anchor to the presentation.

Some of the most dramatic and effective PowerPoint slides use images to represent concepts with minimal use of text. Your slides should enhance your presentation – not detract or distract with busy images or distracting effects. It can also be tempting to use the slides as prompts – resist this as it means you are not focusing on the learners' needs.

✓ BEST FOR

- Most talks and lectures can be made more interesting through the use of visual aids.

✚ MORE

- Create prompts using written notes or the Notes section in PowerPoint. It is possible to display the Notes page on your computer screen while displaying the slideshow to the class on a larger screen. This is known as Presenter View (see http://office.microsoft.com/en-us/powerpoint-help/view-your-speaker-notes-privately-while-delivering-a-presentation-on-multiple-monitors-HA010067383.aspx for further detail).

- Take a final look at your presentation as if you are in the audience – can you read the screen, are the points clear, what does your spoken input add to the visual element? It is worth checking to see whether your slides can be seen from the back of the room you plan to use: a lot of new presentation spaces have such low ceilings that the bottom half of a screen can be hidden by people sitting at the front of the room!
- Be careful with your use of fonts, colours and backgrounds – ensure they are legible. Sans serif fonts are recommended for slides.
- Keep the number of slides to a minimum.
- Time your presentation – a rule of thumb should be using one slide for four to five minutes (note that this depends on the type of slides you use and how much text is on them). Do not include slides that you will have to skim over.
- If you are switching between your slides and another program, for example a web browser, hold the ALT key and press Tab (CMD and press Tab if you are a Mac user) to easily switch between them.
- To blank out the presentation, just press 'B'. It will return if you touch any key.
- Consider going 'cold turkey' and not using PowerPoint at all for your presentation. You might find your audience pays more attention to what you are saying. They will certainly look at you more which can take some getting used to!
- Try a web-based presentation tool such as Prezi (http://prezi.com). You could also create and display a mind map, devise a web page, use a flip chart or go retro and try an old-fashioned overhead projector.
- Use a tablet PC or an interactive whiteboard to 'draw' on your slides, or draw from scratch (e.g. a Venn diagram to explain Boolean searching). This is a modern-day version of using acetates and an overhead projector, but the effect can be refreshing compared to static PowerPoint slides.
- Consider using a hand-held remote control to move slides on. This frees you up to move away from the presentation computer to engage more with your learners.

❗ WATCH OUT

- Remember you do not have to use PowerPoint just for the sake of it. If you can speak clearly and in a structured way without preparing slides, try it out. You might find that talking to your learners and supplying a handout with any technical detail works just as well and in fact gives you a little more freedom.

42 Practical preparation

In order for your teaching to be successful, you need to be prepared. As well as getting your content ready, there are other practical issues to be considered. Whether you teach regularly or once in a while, it is a good idea to create a checklist of items so you can be certain nothing is forgotten. When preparing for sessions, *never assume anything* – always double check!

✓ BEST FOR

- every kind of learning and teaching opportunity.

✚ MORE

Items you may want to include on a checklist are:

- What time can you access the room to prepare?
- Do you have access to the room? Do you need keys or a keycode?
- Do you have all your printed materials? If you have several handouts, include these in your checklist.
- Do you have your electronic files and anything else you need for your presentation?
- Is the room layout appropriate?
- Are you familiar with fire procedures and fire exits?
- Do you know where the toilets are?
- Are there refreshments? If so, where and when will they be delivered? Who do you contact if they do not arrive?
- Is there appropriate signposting to the teaching room?
- Do you need to book travel and hotel accommodation?
- Do you have a list of attendees?
- Do you have logins for the learners' computers?
- Do you have contact details for technical support?

- Is the correct software (including web plug-ins) and hardware available?
- What backup do you have if one computer will not work, or if your file is corrupted?
- Do you have any additional resources you require for your session, e.g. pens, post-its, markers, gluesticks, etc. It may be worth making up a 'kit' of items to take to every session.

! WATCH OUT

- Remember that plans are worthless but planning is everything (Eisenhower, 1957). Plan for the unexpected and be flexible rather than sticking rigidly to a plan. Preparation will always pay dividends.

Reference

Eisenhower, D. D. (1957) *Columbia World of Quotations* (1996), Columbia University Press.

43 Presenting and performing

Remember that each teaching session you run, especially if it is in front of a group, is a performance. Everyone has a different performing style, and you should not try to be someone that you are not. Irrespective of your personal style you will need to find a way to keep the learners' attention and interest. You may have delivered a session many times before, but it will be new for the learners and they will not want or expect to see a teacher who is clearly not very engaged.

You need empathy with your audience to pick up on how they are reacting to you and your content. This requires clear thinking, good planning and a learner-centric view of teaching. There are some simple tricks to improve your performance. For example, try to start well – get your learners' attention quickly by shutting the door, turning on the presentation or stopping something (music perhaps). Make sure that your first sentence is clear and welcoming and certainly do not start with a moan about the room, people being late, and so on. (see **Managing sessions – the start** for further tips on making an impact at the beginning of your sessions).

✓ BEST FOR

- giving presentations or lectures.

+ MORE

- Speak in sentences and be clear. Presenting is not like having a conversation with friends so do not let sentences fade away or make assumptions that people will finish off the sentence themselves. This is especially true when teaching learners whose first language is not English.
- Make eye contact with your audience: this makes them feel included, but try not to focus on any individual for too long.
- Signpost the session. Say so when you are about to move on to

something new. Begin with an outline summary and finish by concluding key points.

- Arrange for each key point to be put across in three ways – e.g. spoken, onscreen and in a handout.
- Try to pace yourself – most people speed up at the start and end of sessions. Take a deep breath and slow down if necessary.
- Do not attempt to cover too much: pick your key messages and include any extra material in a handout.
- Be comfortable – a workshop is not the place to try out that new pair of shoes!
- Use humour carefully. (See **Jokes and humour**.)
- Allow questions – it is up to you whether you have them during or at the end of the presentation.
- End on time or early – never late. The only reason to finish late is if your learners do not want to leave and you are happy to stay with them. And yes, sometimes that does happen!
- Watch good performers – teachers, actors, comedians or anyone performing – and see what makes them good. Likewise, when you see a bad performance, try to analyse why it did not work.
- Video yourself to see what you look like when you present – this can bring home any bad habits you may have.
- Find your own style: do not feel you have to imitate someone else. For example, if you are not comfortable with jokes, then do not include them!
- Make sure you practice your presentation so you are comfortable with the content and pace. This will also enable you to judge timing accurately. Many presentations are ruined by running out of time and rushing at the end, or they just simply over-run! If possible, practice with a colleague and ask for comments.
- If you use PowerPoint, see **PowerPoint**.
- Be confident. Even if you do not feel it, act confidently!

❖ WATCH OUT

- If you make a mistake, do not worry – often your audience may not have noticed! If necessary, admit your mistakes and errors, but do not try to bluff your way through. Remember, you may have deviated from what you planned to say, but your audience may never know. Simply correct yourself and move on. An audience will find it more awkward to watch you become embarrassed and red-faced rather than just acknowledge the mistake and move on. If necessary, take a moment to compose yourself.

- One of the functions of a teacher is to motivate the learners. No one can be inspirational all of the time, but at the very least try not to demotivate the learners by bringing your problems into the classroom. Remember, the show must go on, no matter how you're feeling.

44 Questions

Questions can be a very powerful tool to enhance and guide learning. By asking effective questions in the right way, you can encourage your learners to think and ensure that they are achieving the learning outcomes.

'Open questions' cannot be answered with a yes or no, and require a fuller answer. They are useful for testing understanding, as they require learners to explain and give in-depth answers. These questions usually start with: Why? How? What? For example: How could you improve that search? What would you do differently?

'Closed questions' have a yes or no answer. They are useful if you want to test whether a learner knows a specific fact but will not give you any other information. They can be used to emphasize a point, for example, asking whether the learners agree with a point of view. However, this would normally need to be combined with an open question in order to explore why they agree or disagree. For example: Did you think that journal was a good source to use? Why?

'Ask, pause and place questions' can make a presentation interactive and test whether the learners have listened to what the teacher has said. If you want to ask a group of learners a question, ask the question first and then pause. Once you have paused for a few seconds, choose the person you want to answer. This means that everyone in the group will try to think of the answer as they will not know who will be asked to answer. If you choose a person first, then ask the question, only the person you have chosen is required to think of an answer. For example, try: 'When would you use a search engine rather than a library database?', pause, 'Jo?'; rather than: 'Jo, when would you use a search engine rather than a library database?'

You need to forewarn your learners that they will be expected to answer questions as they go along. To spring questions on them may cause some participants to feel uncomfortable.

The following example shows how effectively questioning can be used to develop critical thinking and evaluation. The 'Blooming Blooms' activity is aimed at young children and uses questions related to fairy tales. These questions are mapped to the levels of Bloom's taxonomy (see **Facilitating Learning**). Examples **44.1** and **44.2** give generic questions which can be adapted to any age or topic, followed by an example relating to the fairy-tale 'Goldilocks and the Three Bears'.

....

44.1 *Blooming Blooms – using Blooms Taxonomy to develop questioning*

....

Questions for Remembering
- What happened before ... after...?
- How many ...?
- What is ...?
- Who was it that ...?
- How would you explain ... describe ... show ...?
- When ... why ... how ... did?
- Can you identify ... select ... picture ...?
- Who spoke to ...?
- Who or what were ...?

Questions for Understanding
- How would you say ... tell in your own words?
- How would you explain ...?
- What do you think could have happened next ...?
- Who do you think ...?
- Can you clarify what it means by ...?
- What example(s) could you give of ...?
- What facts or ideas or words show ...?
- How could you explain what is happening and why?

Questions for Applying
- How/why is ... an example of ...?
- What facts would you choose to show ...?
- How would you explain what is happening and why ...?
- What examples can you find to ...?
- Do you know of another instance where ...?
- Can you group by characteristics such as ...?
- Which factors would you change if ...?
- How would you use ...?
- From the information given, can you develop a set of instructions about ...?

Questions for Analysing
- Which events could not have happened?
- If ... happened ... what might have the ending have been?
- What part of the story was the ... funniest? ... saddest? ... most exciting?
- Which things were facts and which opinions?
- What was the purpose of ...?
- What was the important information and what was irrelevant?
- What evidence can you find to ...?

Questions for Evaluating
- Is there a better solution to ...?
- Judge the value of ...? What do you think ...?
- Can you defend your position about ...?
- Do you think ... is a good or bad thing?
- How would you have handled ...?
- What changes to ... would you recommend?
- Why did they (the character) choose ...?
- Were they right to do so ...?
- What are the consequences ...?
- What would you say is the importance of ...?
- What are the pros and cons of ...?
- Why is ... of value?
- What are the alternatives?
- What would you recommend?
- Was the main character in the story good or bad? Why?

Questions for Creating
- Suppose you could ... what would you do?
- What would be a possible solution to ...?
- How could you change the plot?
- How could you design/invent a new way to ...?
- How would you explain ... describe ... show...?
- What theory can you come up with for ...?
- What new and unusual uses can you think of for ...?
- What proposal can you come up with for ...?
- What outcome could you predict if ...?

Katrina Little, Kilmacolm Nursery, 2009

44.2 Blooming Blooms example – Goldilocks

Remembering	**the recall of specific information** • Who was Goldilocks? • Where did she live? With whom? • What did her mother tell her not to do?
Understanding	**an understanding of what was read** • This story was about .... (Topic) • The story tells us ....(Main idea) • Why didn't her mother want her to go to the forest? • What did Goldilocks look like? • What kind of girl was she?
Applying	**the converting of abstract content to concrete situations** • How were the bears like real people? • Why did Goldilocks go into the little house? • Write a sign that should be placed near the edge of the forest. • Draw a picture of what the bears' house looked like. • Draw a map showing Goldilocks's house, the path in the forest, the bears' house, etc. • Show through action how Goldilocks sat in the chairs, ate the porridge, etc.
Analysing	**the comparison and contrast of the content: the breaking down of ideas in order to understand the whole thing better** • How did each bear react to what Goldilocks did? • How would you react? • Compare Goldilocks to any friend. • When did Goldilocks leave her real world for fantasy? How do you know?
Evaluating	**the judgement and evaluation of characters, actions, outcome, etc., for personal reflection and understanding** • Why were the bears angry with Goldilocks? • Why was Goldilocks happy to go home? • What do you think she learned by going into that house? • Do you think she will listen to her mother's warnings in the future? Why? • Do parents have more experience and background than their children? • Would you have gone into the bears' house? Why or why not? • Do you think this really happened to Goldilocks? Why? • Why would a grown-up write this story for children to read? • Why has the story of Goldilocks been told to children for many, many years?

Creating	**the organization of thoughts, ideas and information from the content**
	• List the events of the story in sequence.
	• Point out the importance of time sequence words by asking:
	  — What happened after Goldilocks ate the Baby Bear's porridge?
	  — What happened before Goldilocks went into the forest?
	  — What is the first thing she did when she went into the house?
	• Draw a cartoon or stories about bears. Do they all act like humans?
	• Do you know any other stories about little girls or boys who escaped from danger?
	• Make a puppet out of one of the characters. Using the puppet, act out his/her part in the story.
	• Make a model of the bears' house and the forest.
	
	Katrina Little, Kilmacolm Nursery

✓ BEST FOR

- formative assessment (i.e. assessing learning as you are going along)
- summative assessment (at the end of the session: have they achieved the learning outcomes?)
- making a presentation interactive
- keeping your learners on their toes!

✚ MORE

- You can provide a list of questions on a handout and ask learners to use them to test their own knowledge and understanding.
- Questioning approaches can work very well in online environments, either through synchronous or asynchronous discussions, as frames for activities (similar to using a handout in face-to-face teaching) or as tutor feedback before assessment.

❗ WATCH OUT

- Using the wrong question type can mean you do not find out what knowledge the learners have acquired.
- Avoid leading questions or trying to catch out or put down your learners. E.g. Did you get irrelevant results because you used the wrong technique?

➜ REFERENCE

Irvine, C. (2010) *Quetioning – Kilmacolm's Innovative Blooming Blooms Approach*, National Information literacy Framework Scotland case study, http//caledonianblogs.net/nilfs/2010/02/25/questioning-Kilmacolms-innovative-blooming-blooms-approach.

Acknowledgement

Many thanks to Katrina Little at Kilmacolm Nursery for permission to include her resources.

45 Room layout

Planning your room layout will have a very positive effect on any learning and teaching event, and change the impact of anything you do. Here are some suggestions:

- The ballroom/cabaret style uses round tables and chairs placed throughout the room. This is not always comfortable if you have your back to the stage, but is good for group interaction (as long as the tables are not too big and the facilitator is easy to see and hear).
- Blended classrooms use flexible layouts and have access to IT. You can move furniture to create a mixture of working environments. You may need to think about programs to control computers if the space is diverse, as learners could become distracted.
- The boardroom style is where the whole class sits around a table (e.g. a long rectangle or U-shaped layout). This is good for discussion and interaction with the teacher/facilitator.
- A circle or semicircle layout is also useful for discussion and interaction.
- Empty space is handy for creative improvisation, but you may need to think very carefully how you will use it.
- If using an IT lab with computers and desks in rows, you may need to consider how important group work or non-IT work might be. Computers can create a barrier between you and your learners so it may be more difficult to build a rapport with them while presenting in this room layout.
- A lecture-style layout where all the chairs face the front is useful for listening to the teacher and watching demonstrations, but not very good for group work. The teacher controls this environment, and has eye contact with everyone.
- Sitting in a lounge-style on easy chairs can be useful for discussions or tutorials, but it is not always easy to write or make things in this layout.
- The World Café (www.theworldcafe.com) layout is like a ballroom but with paper tablecloths you use to write your ideas on. This layout is good for mind mapping. Participants usually move between tables.

You should think about access to technology: check that everyone can see the main screen easily. Try out seats around the room and check for acoustics and sightlines – especially whether pillars or other equipment are in the way. Check whether the screen is too low or if it is in full sunlight. There is relatively cheap screen control software available that will allow you to take control of individual PCs and display your presentation, thus reducing the need for learners to follow the main screen in an IT lab. If you are using flip charts, whiteboards or other screens, then follow the same checks as for technology.

Tables are useful if you want learners to be able to take notes or work on something. They do, however, present a barrier and this can lead learners to fall back into a comfort zone and not contribute as much as possible. Look into flexible furniture – tables on wheels are relatively common and can be pulled into the appropriate configuration very quickly.

Think about works best for you – do you move around or do you prefer to stay close to a podium? If the former, make sure that you have space to do so. This is particularly important in computer labs.

✓ BEST FOR

- all kinds of learning and teaching events.

✚ MORE

- Experiment with different layouts for different purposes. It is easy to accept whatever fate gives you but just as you would try different techniques, try different layouts.
- Think about the control you want and need to have. You will often not have control over the room, or if you do, you may have to follow another class that has moved furniture into a configuration that is not your preferred one. Can you allow the learners to move the room into a configuration that suits them? Maintaining eye contact with all the learners is important, so check the sightlines from the presenter's viewpoint too. Spaces away from your eyeline can quickly turn into 'naughty corners'.

❗ WATCH OUT

- Is the room layout absolutely necessary for the learning outcomes to be achieved? If you can guarantee control over the layout then this is acceptable, but otherwise it is a very high-risk strategy as facilities are often limited in their flexibility.
- Make sure that you leave space for those with mobility problems (such as wheelchair access).

46 Teaching assistants

Using a teaching assistant is different to team teaching in that the teaching assistant is a junior partner. This is particularly useful when teaching large groups or teaching in computer labs. Use your partner – perhaps a graduate trainee or paraprofessional – to hand out material, circulate the room helping with and/or facilitating group or individual work, fix password problems, and so on. This frees you from much of the routine that can slow down the session and allows more flexible and developmental activity. It can also provide an excellent activity for new or inexperienced teachers who will benefit from observing you teach at close hand but also begin to engage with learners directly.

✓ BEST FOR

- large groups
- computer labs
- developing staff.

+ MORE

- Use learners who have already taken the session to help. These could be students helping those in years below them or learners wishing to reinforce their own learning – the most effective way to embed information is to teach it to others.

⦂ WATCH OUT

- Assistants need to be well briefed on the session and should feel some ownership of the activities that you are asking them to contribute to. If they do not feel involved they may well demotivate learners as they struggle to follow your thinking.
- Be clear of boundaries in approach. Assistants should never contradict or

argue with you unless they have clear permission to do so (a debate can encourage an open atmosphere in the session if handled well, but it should have parameters and a rationale).

47 Team teaching

Team teaching refers to running a learning/teaching event with one or more colleagues. This can work in a number of ways.

The most common form of team teaching is pairing up with someone else to share the running of a single session, workshop or class, so the event is led by two people rather than one. The term 'team teaching' also applies when different teachers lead a series of classes, or when there are parallel classes taking place with similar content but different teachers.

Team teaching has a number of advantages over teaching solo, but it is resource-intensive and doubles the amount of staff time dedicated to your teaching activity – you may need to check that this approach can be justified.

Team teaching has advantages for both the teachers and the learners. From the learner's perspective, a session led by more than one teacher brings variety and often increases interaction. When the session has a lot of tutor input, team teaching brings variation in tone, emphasis, speaking style and language. When there are learner activities, team teaching increases the opportunities for expert support and advice, enabling one tutor to work with a small group of learners without fearing that the rest of the class is being ignored.

As a teacher, team teaching can be very valuable for a range of reasons. Sharing the running of a session can be less tiring. This is especially true when running a longer course and with a demanding and diverse group of learners. It is also a powerful developmental approach, building up peer support and creating opportunities for informal peer observation (so you and your colleague learn from each other and build up confidence).

The other forms of team teaching share some of the above advantages. In particular, they reduce the burden on an individual and share the work out between colleagues. In a lot of library and information environments this can be particularly helpful in developing the whole of the teaching team, meaning that teaching commitments can be covered if for some reason the person supposed to be leading the session is not available.

✓ BEST FOR

- large groups
- courses rather than one-off sessions.

✚ MORE

- Work with different colleagues and see how your teaching persona develops. It is good to have a comfortable double act, but varying your partner can revitalize a session that was getting stale.

❢ WATCH OUT

- Co-delivery often takes longer than working solo, as both teachers might want to speak. Make sure you factor this in when planning the lesson.
- Planning together is very important. It shows all too clearly when someone has been drafted in to help at the last minute. Make sure that you both understand where each will take the lead – confusion can be laughed off once if you are lucky, but if it happens more than once then learners will simply see people who don't know what they are doing and thus lose all confidence.
- Plan how you will signal to each other that you have something to say – it is easy to interrupt and disrupt your colleague's flow.
- Some people simply cannot work together – the chemistry isn't there. Peer observation can be a useful part of team teaching but it can be useful to get an independent observer to critically appraise the teaching team from outside.

48 Technical problems

Most teaching sessions now involve the use of technology, whether for accessing electronic information sources, or using PowerPoint or other programs to give a presentation. Technical problems are an unavoidable hazard. They can undermine your teaching session as learners may not have confidence in the source you are demonstrating. Thorough preparation can help minimize these problems, but flexibility is essential.

✓ BEST FOR

- minimizing the impact of technical problems.

+ MORE

- Ensure you are prepared with guest logins for the computers and websites that may require them. Never rely on your learners bringing their own login: there will always be some who forget.
- Take screen-shots of key demonstrations so if you have network problems you can still deliver a presentation.
- If you are using PowerPoint, print a copy of the presentation in case you cannot access the file. Also, print handouts of the slides so learners can still follow your talk.
- Consider what you would do if the network or website you planned to use went down – can you prepare a different activity as a backup?
- Keep calm if you encounter problems, and try to think of a way to buy some time to work out a solution, e.g. taking a coffee break).
- Do not worry if something unexpected happens during a demonstration, try to make it part of the learning experience.
- Check that the computers have the right hardware and software. Write a list of the programs you use and list these as part of the technical requirements for your session. Do you need to use audio or video? Do you need headphones for participants? Thoroughly detail everything

you need for your session.

- Do not forget to check plug-ins for websites. Many sites require additional plug-ins to view the web content. Make sure these are available in your teaching room.

❗ WATCH OUT

- Expect to have to deal with technical problems, however technically adept you are or whether you are teaching in a brand-new, sophisticated teaching lab. The key to success is to keep calm and don't spend too much time trying to fix it yourself. Remember that every minute you spend trying to reboot, reload or simply cursing is time lost for the learners. Prepare alternative things to do or simply postpone until you can secure technical help.

49 Timing

Timing your session is crucial to its success. When planning the inputs and activities for your teaching, you should time each one. If it over-runs your allotted time, cut something and do not try to force everything to work by shaving minutes off an activity in the hope that it will take less time. Do not try to cram too many slides into your presentation (on average, one slide every four to five minutes is sufficient) and do not underestimate the time it takes for learners to arrange themselves into pairs or groups, to write feedback or to complete exercises. Remember, they will be less sure of the material than you are, so make some allowances for this.

If possible, run through a session beforehand (working perhaps from your lesson plan) but include some activities in your planning that can be added and subtracted from the session if you find it over-running or finishing early. A useful tip is to include a slot at the end of the lesson for a plenary session or questions – this can be cut if you are running badly over (you can deal with questions or problems by allowing them during the session or by following them up later).

Be flexible with your timing during the teaching session, too. If you have set an exercise and the group have finished (or worse, become bored with it!) quicker than you expected, do not be afraid to retain their interest by moving on to something new.

✓ BEST FOR

- all teaching.

✚ MORE

- Be flexible and respond to your learners. Do not plough on with your pre-prepared material if it is clearly unnecessary, as this is a waste of time.

⁝ WATCH OUT

- Most people start very quickly through nerves or excitement so you may find that you have covered more material than expected after the first ten minutes or so. Allow for this in your planning, but also be aware of the possibility and try to make a more measured start to the session.
- Although very few people will complain if you finish a session early, you will certainly be criticized for over-running.

50 Unresponsive participants

All teachers will be faced at some point with unresponsive groups or individuals, who will not answer questions or who will do the bare minimum to get through the learning event. This may have a number of causes – previous experience of information skills teaching, their experiences immediately before your session, poor group dynamics, social activities the night before or simply that your session is boring. The roots of the problem should be explored but more immediate solutions are listed below:

- Ask for one volunteer to do your keyboarding (you may have to choose, in which case take someone from the back row). This will mean that the rest of the group's attention is engaged (in probably waiting for their colleague to fail!). Your demands on the volunteer should not be onerous. It is a good idea to write out the words that you would like entered on a flip chart or whiteboard in case your volunteer is dyslexic.
- Break up the group. There are fewer places to hide in smaller groups and you can then circulate to prompt input.
- Have an activity that you can inject into the session. Physical movement, even if it is just to rearrange the chairs or move into groups, will help energize people.
- Do not make comments about the lack of response – this will almost certainly be seen as a sign of weakness and reinforce their behaviour.
- Do not be sarcastic or cutting if you direct a question to an unresponsive party, especially to an individual. The group may laugh but they will be waiting for your scorn to fall on them and this will not encourage further participation.
- Use a range of active learning techniques to ensure learners are engaged – they are less likely to be unresponsive if you have put some thought into making your session interesting and interactive.

✓ BEST FOR

- any group that may include unresponsive participants.

✚ MORE

- Liaise with others who teach, or are otherwise engaged with, the group to find out if the relevant individuals usually behave like this. If not, then this may signal that your teaching is part of the problem.

❢ WATCH OUT

- Do not panic – you need to stay in control of your teaching. React calmly and if you continue to get no response to your requests for input, either continue with a different delivery style or cut the session short.
- If you call individuals to 'volunteer' for something then be careful that they will not be humiliated by a failure. Asking learners to spell difficult words, or asking them to spell at all if they are dyslexic, can cause real distress.

Activities

51 Action learning

Action learning is an educational process based on working on something 'real', rather than a fictional case study or scenario. It is a type of experiential learning (learning by doing) based on the idea that learning is more effective when dealing with real-life situations and problems. It is also a form of social learning where learners work in groups called 'action learning sets'. Action learning is often associated with the workplace and usually takes place over a period of months, but the general principles can be adapted and applied elsewhere.

Action learning was pioneered by Professor Reg Revans in the UK and is based around the formula $L = P + Q$ (learning = programmed knowledge + questioning). Although Revans did not recommend the use of a coach or tutor to guide the learning set, in practice this is what tends to happen in order to ensure adequate reflection and action takes place. Questioning is particularly important – the tagline of the US-based International Foundation for Action Learning (IFAL, www.ifal.org.uk and www.ifal-usa.org) is 'managing the unknown through questioning'.

Ask your learners to work in small groups – this has been found to be more effective than pairs. The groups may have a joint project they can work on, or each individual can present their own problem. By working together the group pools common knowledge and experience and uses this to address the problem. Through interaction and questioning (from within the group or from a tutor), this should lead to strategies to begin working on a solution. As Pedler (1997) states, 'the learning dynamic is a recognition of a common ignorance'. This is highly relevant to information skills teaching as learners often struggle with scoping their information needs, that is, identifying what they know, what they don't know and what they need to find out.

To begin with you are likely to need to work closely with the sets, in providing knowledge but especially in asking questions. Learners may need to become familiar with types of question in order to explore a problem. As the set develops, they should be able to take more responsibility for the processes and actions.

At the beginning of an action learning set it is helpful that the facilitator either uses or encourages participants to use questioning effectively. The purpose of questioning is to help guide learners to their own conclusions – action learning is not a directive, tutor-centric approach, and effective learning sets are democratic and collaborative rather than serving the needs, desires and opinions of one dominant individual. Participants and the facilitator need to ask open questions – closed, yes-or-no-type questions will not do.

Learners need to examine the problem, asking questions such as: What factors affect the problem, internal and external? Who is involved? What might the cause be? What possible solutions can be tried?

A key question for action learning is: 'What did I learn?' If you want to analyse this question further, try asking: 'What would I do differently, what worked and what did not?'

Action learning is normally best suited to groups you may see over a long period of time, so the group can have the opportunity to carry out new practices and review their success. In reality, most information skills sessions are 'one-offs' with learners working on their own individual projects. However, the key principles can still be applied: the idea of working on a real-life problem, social learning and the use of questioning to encourage reflection and learning.

✓ BEST FOR

- making learning relevant
- working on real-life problems.

✚ MORE

- Use an action learning approach to develop a collaborative project, such as an essay, a presentation, a website or a report requiring the learners to demonstrate planning, search and evaluation skills.
- See the tip **Questions** tip to learn more about the use of questions in teaching.

❡ WATCH OUT

- A group of individuals working on their own activities can be demanding for the teacher, as each person may need a lot of attention. Keep groups small, ask learners to help each other, or draft in colleagues to help with the session.

- Effective questioning is the key to making action learning work. You will need to observe questioning practice and provide very careful briefings and lots of support on this process.

→ FURTHER READING

CIPD Action Learning Factsheet,
  www.cipd.co.uk/subjects/lrnanddev/general/actionlearning.htm.
Pedler, M. (ed.) (1997) *Action Learning in Practice*, 3rd edn, Gower.

52 Amplifying your teaching

Amplified teaching uses social media to extend the learning and teaching event more actively to all participants within and beyond a single physical location and the designated course attendees.

Event amplification is now ubiquitous, with the greatest volumes of coverage around major political events, celebrity news and controversial television programmes. In the library and information sector context, popular demonstrations in defence of libraries have been amplified (so participants in a sit-in are Tweeting what is happening or uploading their video diaries). On a more day-to-day level, some form of amplification is common at professional conferences or even unconferences (participant-driven meetings that do not follow a standard conference format).

The first step in doing this successfully is to assign a clear, unambiguous name to the session. If using Twitter, this will need to be in the form of a hashtag (#), which is usually an acronym for an event; for example, #lat10 for 'Librarians as Teachers 2010'. Preferably, keep such tags short, as they will use up valuable character space in Tweets. Amplification can be achieved in a number of ways:

Recording the event

- **Amplification of the teacher's input**: using video and audio streaming technologies can make it possible for anyone not physically present in a classroom to hear what the teacher is saying. This is often most effective when the teacher's input is in the form of a talk or lecture, but it can also be used for question and answer sessions. It can be less effective in open discussions or workshops. This is very often used at large conferences. Sometimes you may need to pay a fee to subscribe to any live streaming.
- **Amplification of the teacher's slides and any written output**: any slides or presentation content can be made available via the conference website (sometimes for a fee), via a global repository service for presentations, such as SlideShare (www.slideshare.net), or within a Virtual Learning

Environment (VLE) (also known as a Learning Management System or LMS).

- **Amplification across time**: the lecture or talk can be made available for a finite or undefined period by using podcasting or videocasting and by maintaining an archive copy.

Interactivity and discussion

- **Amplification of feedback to the speaker**: micro-blogging, i.e. Tweeting, can be used as a discussion channel for conference participants and as a way of providing real-time feedback to the teacher. For example, a screen with the relevant Twitter stream can be made available near the speaker, thus providing immediate feedback and helping to shape the teacher's input.
- **Amplification of resources**: participants can be encouraged to make their own contribution to the discussion within a class or workshop using collaborative technologies. This might be in the form of discussions on Twitter, or within a VLE; but many other types of media could be used, including using photographs (posted on Twitter, Facebook, Flickr or any other suitable platform), blogs or videos. The role of the teacher will often shift to a facilitator role, as learners become producers of learning resources. For this to happen effectively, you probably need a longer session, or for your amplified event to take place over a period of time.

Extending the event

- **Amplification of an audience's collective memory**: participants can use Twitter or Flickr, for example, to create a record of the learning and teaching event. This can be especially useful if it is a special event such as the end of a course with learner presentations, a guest speaker or some kind of debate.
- **Amplification of participation**: involvement in the learning and teaching event can extend beyond those able to be there in person or who are registered on the course. Other learners can participate in the event by following discussions on social networks and sending in their own contributions.
- **Amplification of resources**: you can reference or link to selected learning resources; participants might check them out following links from any live streaming.

✓ BEST FOR

- In a teaching situation, it is probably best to have some kind of strong and interesting event as the basis for your amplification. It could be a lecture – just be sure that participants will use a social medium to engage in a debate.
- Engaging learners in debate and discussion.

✚ MORE

- Event amplification can be very powerful. As well as challenging the relationship between teacher and learners (an area which is much discussed in the shift from teacher to learning facilitator), it can extend participation within and beyond the classroom. It may be that some learners prefer to comment using some form of social media, whereas they would not speak in a lecture room.
- More significantly, event amplification can be a very effective way of drawing in participation from a much wider audience. It might be a way of engaging university students in a discussion with local residents, drawing in perspectives from other communities and cultures, or getting feedback from people you may not have contacted yourself. Currently, many journalists follow amplified events, so you may pick up wider media coverage than you initially expected.

❗ WATCH OUT

- Event amplification will only work if you are working with learners who are engaged with the technology. It would be misguided to try to amplify the first part of a beginner's guide to the internet, for example, although it might be worth trying later on.
- You need to consider whether there are any expectations of confidentiality (in terms of content) or workplace restrictions on media use. Amplifying a confidential training course or a session which the speaker has asked to be closed, or in an organization which discourages the use of social media, would be unwise. Use your common sense.

53 Audio feedback

Providing feedback to learners is an essential part of the assessment process but one that is often seen as something outside of the remit of library and information professionals. Feedback to learners is usually associated with written comments on a standard sheet or scribbled in the margins of their work. Because we may not be involved regularly in the formal assessment process, we might therefore consider this part of the learning and teaching process best to be left to others. However, we should be providing feedback to our learners on how they are progressing towards achieving the learning outcomes that we have set, praising or amending as required. (See **Feedback to learners**.)

Much of our feedback will be given verbally during sessions. However, if the opportunity arises to provide feedback after sessions or as part of a formal assessment and feedback process, then audio feedback is a very effective alternative to written comments. In the Sounds Good project, Rotheram (2009a) found that student satisfaction with feedback rose significantly if it was provided via a sound file. The level and amount of feedback given by the tutor also rose with over four or five times more words spoken on the sound file than would usually be written on a sheet. Participants in the project found that recording audio feedback takes no longer than producing written sheets.

The process is simple. Record your comments using an MP3 player (or similar) and save them as a sound file. The files can then be e-mailed to learners or embedded into a blog, wiki or VLE (virtual learning environment). All the learner requires is an MP3 player or a PC with a sound card to hear the individualized feedback.

Some criteria for successful audio feedback have been collated by Steve Bond at LSE (2009) and reproduced here with permission:

- Do not try to make a perfect recording. People pause, stumble, say 'errr' in real life so there's no problem if you do so in the recording. In fact, it may make your feedback more human if you do make mistakes.
- You do not need a script. However, you do need to prepare. Use

assessment criteria as a guide to what you will say.

- Keep it short and to the point. Do not try to cover too much in one recording. Aim for a five-minute maximum.
- Practice makes perfect. It might take a while to record your first few pieces of feedback, but it will get easier and quicker with repetition.
- You do not have to abandon writing altogether. Some things are easier to explain with a drawing or simply an arrow. Combine audio and text to get the best of both worlds.

✓ BEST FOR

- An alternative to written feedback if you are involved in formal assessment
- Giving informal, formative feedback to individuals after a teaching session, or in response to a request for help
- Providing a useful alternative to written feedback to those learners who have accessibility problems with text, including those who are visually impaired or dyslexic.

✚ MORE

- If a group of learners are making the same mistakes, you may wish to record some generic feedback for the whole group in addition to individual feedback.
- Include pictures or a link to a presentation or video clip to make it more interesting to sit and listen to.
- Audio clips can be inserted into Word documents (Insert > Object). This means that feedback can be targeted to specific points in a written document rather than remaining as a separate file. It is also possible to record the audio from within Word rather than embedding an external file (http://office.microsoft.com/en-us/word-help/insert-a-sound-HP005257344.aspx).
- Use free screen capture software such as Screenr (www.screenr.com) or Jing (www.techsmith.com/jing) to record your voice commenting on a learner's work – this links the comments to the work directly.

❗ WATCH OUT

- Be careful to name your files soon after you record them. Unless the feedback is generic in nature, it should be private between tutor and learner. If you are recording a large batch in one go, then files can get mixed up and there is a danger that you might send the comments to the wrong person.

⚬⋄ REFERENCES

Bond, S. (2009) *Audio Feedback*, Centre for Learning Technology, London School of Economics and Political Science, http://eprints.lse.ac.uk/30693/.

Rotheram, B. (2009a) *Sounds Good: final report*, http://sites.google.com/site/soundsgooduk/downloads.

→ FURTHER READING

Rotheram, B. (2009b) *Practice Tips on Using Digital Audio for Assessment Feedback*, http://sites.google.com/site/soundsgooduk/downloads..

54 Bibliographies

Ask your learners to compile a bibliography: finding, identifying, listing and organizing material relevant to a topic or theme. This is a very effective way of developing many aspects of information literacy and in testing skills and knowledge. A bibliography assignment can be set at varying levels of complexity across all levels of education and it can be set as a standalone test or as part of a larger piece of assessment, for example, as a component in a literature review or essay assessment.

Be clear on your parameters before you start the exercise and do not assume that learners will know what a bibliography is. A sample may be useful, especially if you want more than a simple list. Be clear on the referencing scheme that you require your learners to use and provide examples. If the piece is to be assessed summatively, provide clear assessment criteria, such as how many marks for selection of material, how many for referencing, and so on.

✓ BEST FOR

- Learners who will be required to produce bibliographies as part of their core work or, better still, as an element of other marked work. This can work very well in a context when your learners need to build on their knowledge of a particular subject, so a bibliography could be the starting point for an essay, literature review or research project.
- Testing communication and ICT skills through the compilation of the information and the quality of the referencing skills (or use of a relevant software package).
- Providing a very authentic way of assessing a range of information literacy skills, ranging from finding information to critical evaluation and presentation in a holistic way.
- Testing referencing skills in a 'live' situation.

✚ MORE

You might want to try one of the following variations:

- Ask the learners to create a short reading (or resource) list for those new to the selected subject.
- Set an annotated bibliography on a topic (one you set or one of the learner's choice).
- Ask for a bibliography of a particular type of material, e.g. academic journals, to familiarize learners with the information source.
- Develop a wiki-based bibliography that the whole class contributes to and/or amends.
- Base tasks around the use of a reference management software program like RefWorks, EndNote or Zotero (www.refworks.com; www.endnote.com; www.zotero.org).
- Create collaborative bibliographies using CiteULike or Mendeley (www.citeulike.org; www.mendeley.com).
- Do a quick-fire challenge – provide five references and ask the learners to cite them correctly.
- Embed within Problem-Based Learning (PBL), and ensure that referencing is part of the required solution.
- Link to evidence-based practice or a critical appraisal report.
- Group tasks – could be a role assigned within a bigger project.
- Link to a literature review (and discuss).

Think about how to audit whether your bibliography meets external information literacy standards.

An example of a bibliography assignment compared against SCONUL's The Seven Pillars of Information Literacy (2007) is shown in example **54.1**.

❗ WATCH OUT

- If you allow the learners to choose their own subject matter, be careful to check that there will be enough material before you give a final OK – learners often have a touching faith that books and academic articles will be dedicated to their pet project!
- You also need to be aware of the scope for plagiarism, and check when assessing the assignment that the learners have not just pasted in the first items found on a Google search. You should also review carefully the

54.1	
SCONUL (The Seven Pillars of Information Literacy)	How a bibliography meets SCONUL
1. The ability to recognize a need for information	This is perhaps less satisfactory in a bibliography as the need for information is a given within the assignment
2. The ability to distinguish ways in which the information 'gap' may be addressed	The learning outcomes of the bibliography task can incorporate an element that rewards the range and selection of a variety of material
3. The ability to construct strategies for locating information	This can be an explicit assessment component or learning outcome: a listing or discussion of search strategies and sources consulted
4. The ability to locate and access information	Obviously this is a key element of the task: finding material and identifying it correctly. You can also set parameters for the types of sources consulted (Google, academic databases, library catalogue, etc.)
5. The ability to compare and evaluate information obtained from different sources	Selection is also a key element of a bibliography: normally learners should find plenty of material on the given topic and the bibliography should select the most relevant material, based on the assessment criteria. Remember, you can also require your learners to compile a critical, annotated bibliography with a commentary on the items selected
6. The ability to organize, apply and communicate information to others in appropriate ways	A good bibliography is correctly formatted, using a recognized form of referencing. Effective presentation is critical. The assessment criteria can also require that the bibliography is prepared for different audiences, e.g. for members of the public, school students, undergraduates, experts in a subject, etc.
7. The ability to synthesize and build upon existing information, contributing to the creation of new knowledge	This is perhaps a little more problematic unless the level of the bibliography is so comprehensive or definitive that it makes a contribution to the understanding of the subject. This may be particularly possible if you require that the bibliography is critical or evaluative

quality of critical annotations, and check that these have not been cut and pasted from online book reviews or Wikipedia entries.

- Remember that although bibliographies can be very authentic assessments, a basic bibliography without any kind of knowledge context can be a sterile assessment that does not realistically link to other work.
- Think about the kinds of materials and resources that you would like your learners to incorporate. Are you mainly interested in academic resources or can your learners use a wider range of material? Make sure you specify this when setting the bibliography task.

↦ REFERENCE

SCONUL (2007) *The Seven Pillars of Information Literacy Model,* www.sconul.ac.uk/groups/information_literacy/seven_pillars.html.

55 Blogs

A blog is a web log or online diary that has a very simple structure: the owner of the blog writes 'posts' that are dated and displayed with the most recent first, and archived by month. Blogs can be multimedia by incorporating images, audio or video. They can also be interactive through the use of a 'comments' facility whereby other people can post a reaction to a blog post. Most blogs can also be made private, making them visible only to the blog owner and invited guests. A blog will normally have a web feed available, which means other people can 'subscribe' to your blog using an RSS reader – new blog posts will be delivered to the learner without them having to check the blog every day. The simplicity of a blog means that it can be used in many ways, either by the teacher or learner.

There are many websites where you can create a blog, some of which are free and offer good functionality, including Blogger (owned by Google, www.blogger.com) and WordPress (www.wordpress.com). Blog sites vary in the features that they offer and some sites require payment.

Ask learners to use a blog to record their research strategies for a particular project. Encourage reflection on why particular sources were used and ask for links to any online sources to be embedded into the blog. For example, ask what information was found at those sources. What strategies did learners use to find the information? Is the source considered to be a reliable source with good-quality information?

✓ BEST FOR

- encouraging self-reflection
- engaging learners through the use of technology
- encouraging interaction and peer review.

+ MORE

- Set a task where learners write the diary of a historic or fictional figure.

In order to write the diary the learners must research the history of that person.

- Set up a blog yourself to use in teaching sessions. Add resources and encourage exploration and discussion of the resources.
- Use a blog for current awareness, informing learners of new sources or issues relating to information literacy – learners can subscribe to your blog using the RSS feed.
- Look for inspiration at other blogs – there are many different styles of blog (Bhargava, 2010) that you could try for yourself or with learners. For example, including reviews of books or events, interviews, providing opinions on current events, including images or video (useful for exploring visual literacy) – the list is endless!

❗ WATCH OUT

- Do not be despondent if you set up a current awareness blog and you do not receive any comments – people may still be reading it and finding it useful.
- Remember as well that students may take a while to get used to blogging, especially if they are not used to reflective practice. (See **Reflection** for further guidance on developing reflective practice.)

↝ REFERENCE

Bhargava, R. (2010) *The 25 Basic Styles of Blogging … And When To Use Each One*, http://blog.ogilvypr.com/2007/04/157.

→ FURTHER READING

Payne, G. (2008) Engage or Enrage: the blog as an assessment tool. In Godwin, P. and Parker J. (eds), *Information Literacy Meets Web 2.0*, Facet Publishing.

56 Brainstorming

Brainstorming is a simple and effective activity that requires little equipment and can, if executed properly, energize a group. It can also, however, fall flat if no one contributes, so always make it relevant to the group (generic brainstorms barely ever work) and have your own words ready in case it fails to spark interest.

It can be used in a variety of contexts but one obvious use in information literacy is to generate keywords. Always use the words that you gather – enter them into a database as part of a demonstration perhaps – as this will make the exercise immediately relevant. This will be enhanced if the topic is something that your learners need to research. If the latter is the case and the group has access to a VLE or social networking site, then post the results of the brainstorm there. Some useful work can come out of these exercises but it is rarely captured other than at the time.

Brainstorms can be used at the start of a session to find out about a group's knowledge, experience and attitude. For example, have a quick brainstorm on the sources of information learners would use for a specific project and why. This helps you gauge their knowledge and also allows you to tailor your content. Brainstorms can also be provocative. For example, ask learners what they think of libraries – this could be good or bad. You can then challenge their expectations.

If the group is very quiet, and you suspect that they will not call out words, you might want to split them into smaller groups to work on their keywords or ideas and then pool the group efforts. Try not to pick on individuals unless they are keen to contribute. Encourage contributions by making the brainstorm relevant and interesting, but if all fails then ask for contributions from 'all those in blue' or 'people on the second row' rather than individuals.

✓ BEST FOR

- group work
- involving learners in a lecture theatre

- making search strategies relevant.

✚ MORE

You can brainstorm using:

- Learners calling out with presenter noting words on a flip chart or whiteboard
- Groups brainstorming and then pooling
- Synchronous or asynchronous brainstorming via an online discussion board, blog or wiki
- Learners writing on sticky notes and sticking them on a board.

Use a poster tour format to have several simultaneous brainstorms happening with learners building on each other's work as they progress around the posters (see **Poster tours**).

❗ WATCH OUT

- The uncertainties of group dynamics mean that you will almost certainly fail to elicit any input from some groups. If the topic is relevant and you have placed it clearly into context, then this should be rare. However, when it does happen, move on – have examples ready to use and carry on, as facing the group down will achieve little but frustration on your part.
- Some people do not like the term 'brainstorm' so you may come across alternative terms like 'thought shower'.

➜ FURTHER READING

Proctor, T. (2005) *Creative Problem Solving for Managers*, 2nd edn, Routledge, 118–37.

57 Building blocks

This tip is an interactive method of teaching learners how to create search queries. Instead of working on paper or a computer, learners use cards as 'building blocks' to construct their queries. This activity would normally follow on from an explanation of different search techniques and be used to consolidate and test understanding.

Start by preparing a sample search that demonstrates the strategies you wish to teach. Write the keywords and search operators on cards or sheets of paper – operators may include AND, OR, NOT for traditional Boolean searching, or you may wish to use search-engine syntax such as the plus and minus signs. Make duplicate cards of search operators in case they need to be used more than once. Break your search down into simple steps, for example, starting with a simple query, such as connecting two keywords using 'AND' and build the query step by step. Give the cards out to learners and ask them to arrange the cards into a query that matches what you have asked for. Using cards enables elements of the search to be rearranged easily.

This is a very flexible and interactive technique, which can be used on desks/tables or in a more active way on flipcharts and walls. Getting learners on their feet and moving around energizes a session and encourages group discussion. The exercise can be adapted easily to be used with groups of varying numbers and for learners of different levels.

✓ BEST FOR

- energizing group sessions
- use with varying numbers and learners of different levels.

+ MORE

- Use small cards or post-it notes on a table for small groups, pairs or individual activities. Give feedback to each individual/group.
  Alternatively, ask learners to stick their cards on flip-chart paper on the

wall and ask the rest of the group to give feedback before giving your own feedback.

- This activity can be used to liven up presentations to large groups. Use larger sheets of paper or card and use the same technique described above, using volunteers at the front of the group. Engage the group by asking for feedback on the strategies the volunteers create.
- Depending on the level of your students, you can adapt this activity to use the cards to 'fill in the blanks' rather than construct the strategy from scratch.
- Use different coloured cards for the elements of the search strategy (keywords, operators, brackets, etc.). This provides a visual stimulus but also helps clarify the elements of the search.

❗ WATCH OUT

- When using this activity, be careful about the group size you use – you may find that if the group is too large, they may find it difficult to agree on an order. An alternative is to ask one or two individuals to direct and arrange the group.

58 Buzz groups

Buzz groups can be an effective alternative to brainstorming as a way of involving learners and breaking up a lecture. Set a topic for discussion and ask the learners to discuss it with the person next to them. After a few moments they should in turn discuss it with the pair sitting in front or behind them, and so on. Stop when you judge it practical to do so (usually when the group size reaches eight), and ask for feedback from the groups that have formed.

Topics that you could try this with might include:

- Evaluating particular types of information – give the groups a type of information source to look at (say an academic article) and discuss their strengths and weaknesses.
- Creating lists of keywords for a search.
- Pulling together a number of things that have caused problems in their information searching. You can then take these and work with them over the rest of the session.

✓ BEST FOR

- tiered lecture theatres, as people can turn around and talk to those above them in the tier
- sharing experiences and opinions
- getting contributions from all group members.

✦ MORE

- Ask the pairs to write down their thoughts and then pass them to another pair for discussion and comment. They add their comments to the paper and it is passed on to another group.
- Ask learners to come up with three things that drive them mad about the library or three things that have frustrated them about finding information. They will need to restrict the list to three items in order to

negotiate with the other pairs when they combine, but this can give you some really useful information about your services or about the knowledge level of your learners.

❗ WATCH OUT

- It can be easy for the groups to lose focus as they join up, especially if they are not familiar with one another – they will need to introduce themselves and/or overcome any shyness about sharing before they can start work each time. There is also likely to be a lot of repetition when groups join together. Set clear instructions on how the buzz groups should work and impose quite tight time constraints on each element.
- Group size can be difficult to gauge at times, and will also be determined to some extent by the topic. If it is controversial then there will be scope for debate. Finding keywords to describe a topic will probably run out of steam fairly quickly. In a lecture theatre it is probably best to stop at two pairs collaborating, but you can let the groups grow bigger if the environment is amenable.
- Keep an eye on timings – make a judgement based on the level of conversation (noise and content) before you ask groups to combine.

59 Card sorting

A set of blank cards can be a simple yet effective teaching tool. Many learners struggle with how to think of appropriate keywords and construct search strategies using synonyms and related words – this technique can help.

First, ask your learners to identify a search topic. Then, ask them to use the cards to note words that relate to that topic – use a single card per topic. Ask them to think about as many alternative words as possible. After ten minutes or so, stop and run a feedback session – you can then review the cards and reflect on the use of language and synonyms. Ask the learners for alternative words at this point.

Once the group has amassed a collection of words, ask them to start grouping the words into related concepts. The search terms can then be reviewed to discuss which would be the more effective words, and which would work best in a search engine or structured bibliographic database. Explain how to combine the different concepts.

✓ BEST FOR

- developing an understanding of how to break down a search
- choosing appropriate keywords.

✚ MORE

- Extend the activity by including how words from the different groups or concepts can be combined, using, for example, Boolean operators. Consider using the **Building blocks** technique.

❗ WATCH OUT

- Keep this activity simple. It could become complicated and end up discouraging your learners from a more structured approach to searching ('What's the point of this? I can just put a couple of words into Google and it works!'). Be prepared with a few examples of how appropriate word choice makes for a more effective search. You may need to think quite carefully about the subjects/topic areas with which you are working, and make sure that this approach will guarantee better research outcomes.

60 Case studies

Case studies are both a useful teaching tool and an assessment method. They place knowledge in context and this can be particularly effective when dealing with vocational learners or staff development.

Creating case studies can be time-consuming but they will repay the effort if done well. Think of scenarios that will resonate with learners and tell a story. For a case study to work properly it will need to include options – paths that the reader could take to reach an appropriate goal. You will need to end with questions like: 'What should x do?' or: 'What would happen if...?' This should spark discussion in class or online and/or provide an opportunity for a piece of assessed work.

Examples that could be worked up into case studies might include:

- Strategies for finding information for particular purposes – anything from a dissertation to getting legal advice.
- A discussion of what information literacy actually means – useful to get learners to understand their own skills and, more usefully, their skills gaps.
- The effective teaching of information skills to others – teaching others, or in this case planning the teaching of others, is a really effective way of learning.

✓ BEST FOR

- staff development
- vocational students
- students who use case studies in other contexts (such as business).

+ MORE

- One alternative strategy would be to ask your learners to construct a case study from a number of facts. This could illustrate how information is used in the workplace or demonstrate the consequences of an action. This could involve the whole class rather than just individuals or small groups and could be managed via a wiki or similar online tool (such as Google Docs, https://docs.google.com).

- Use the Critical Incident Technique (CIT). CIT uses real-life experience as the basis for learning. More specifically, it involves looking at a significant (or 'critical') experience and exploring this in more detail to identify lessons to be learned. CIT is often used in a strategic context to identify 'critical' incidents, but when used in a teaching context it can provide an effective starting point for the discussion of a case study. You can ask your learners to think of an example of a critical incident, or provide an example of your own.

  There are four key stages to CIT:
  — description of a specific event
  — an account of the learner's actions in the incident
  — what was the outcome?
  — what was the cause?

  This technique could be used for search strategies, encouraging reflection on the use of particular search techniques and sources. For example, you could ask learners to reflect on a recent project or assignment. What information was needed and how did they go about finding it. Where did things go right and wrong? Case study examples from health, law or business where decisions were made on inaccurate or out-of-date information could provide a useful real-life approach.

  CIT can be very useful at engaging learners through using relevant experience, encouraging learners to exchange knowledge and skills, finding out the skill levels and experiences of the learners, developing their understanding of complexity and the impact of their choices in achieving effective learning outcomes. CIT is also effective in encouraging reflective skills. You can use this technique on a one-to-one basis for more in-depth coaching.

⁞ WATCH OUT

- The best case studies are very simple but it is easy to get carried away with them and over-complicate. Try to stick to one or two key points and questions for each case. You'll also need to give clear instructions – many disciplines do not use case studies and although they will be familiar for, say, business students, they will probably be unfamiliar as a tool for those studying the humanities.

- Drawing on real-life experiences can be unpredictable and requires confidence on the part of the teacher. If you do not feel up to dealing with unknown 'critical incidents', perhaps you can research some in advance.

→ FURTHER READING

Flanaghan, J.C. (1954) The Critical Incident Technique, *Psychological Bulletin*, **51**, 327–58.

61 Cephalonian method

The Cephalonian method is a technique for delivering induction sessions to large audiences using a mix of interactive questioning, colour and music. It was developed by Nigel Morgan and Linda Davies (2004) at Cardiff University and is based on a technique used at a welcome session on a package holiday in Cephalonia, Greece. This method involves the use of trigger questions – planted questions that encourage learner participation.

The first step in this technique is to create a set of questions, the answers to which contain all the information you wish to include in your induction session (for example: 'How many books can I borrow?'). First of all you need to decide which topics/questions you want to include and then categorize them into the themes of your presentation. Write the questions on cards, assigning a colour to each category. Then hand out the cards to random members of your audience. During the session, ask for a volunteer to read a question from a particular colour, such as a 'blue question'. Using the colour coding allows the presenter to have some control over the order of the questions, so issues can be addressed in a logical order. After the learner has asked the question, the presenter should locate the appropriate PowerPoint slide and go through that answer. Continue through the 'blue questions' until they are finished, then move on to another colour. Continue this until all the questions have been answered.

✓ BEST FOR

- inductions
- making large 'lecture-type' sessions interactive
- delivering core material in a different way each time
- encouraging participation in large groups where learners may be unwilling to 'expose' themselves by asking a question.

✚ MORE

- Enhance the session by using music while learners enter and leave.

- Ensure the colour is written on the corner of the card – this enables anyone who is colour-blind to identify the appropriate colour.
- You may have to repeat a question once a learner has asked it, as he or she may not speak loud enough for the group to hear.
- Questions could be more involved, such as: 'How can I identify whether a journal is academic or peer-reviewed?'
- Do not use this method as a way of avoiding real questions. Always allow learners to ask supplementary questions or something else relevant to the session. Teaching should be a two-way process. You may want to specify at the start when questions will be taken – during or at the end of your input depending on your preference – as this also gives the group permission to ask them.
- Instead of colour-coded cards you could use numbers or put the cards on particular seats.

❗ WATCH OUT

- Some learners may be reluctant to ask their question, especially if in a large group. If no one is forthcoming, then encourage the person who has the question to give it to someone who is happy to ask it. If this fails, be prepared to ask the question yourself! Keep track of which questions have been asked so you can spot which questions have not.
- Locating the appropriate PowerPoint slide can be tricky and may cause you to trip up. Create a 'key' of questions and note the appropriate slide number next to each question. While in the 'slideshow' view of your presentation, simply type the number of the slide you wish to display and press <Enter> – this will effortlessly take you straight to that slide!
- Be prepared for someone to try and subvert the process by asking a daft question. If they are trying to be clever or to discomfort you then the best way of dealing with these may well be to answer them seriously. If the question is genuinely funny, then laugh and move on.

⟿ REFERENCE

Morgan, N. and Davies, L. (2004) *Innovative Library Induction – Introducing the 'Cephalonian Method'*, SCONUL, www.sconul.ac.uk/publications/newsletter/32/2.rtf.

Acknowledgement

Many thanks to Nigel and Linda at Cardiff University for permission to base this tip on their article.

62 Checklists

A checklist is an informational aid, listing a series of activities to do or questions to answer in order to complete a task. It helps to ensure consistency and completeness in carrying out a task. In many contexts the purpose of checklists is to reduce the risk of failure by listing all the routines that need to be completed rather than relying on human fallibility. Examples of such checklists include those used pre-flight or pre-landing in aviation or in many clinical contexts.

Checklists are an invaluable approach to planning a learning and teaching event. You could draw up a list of all the things you need to consider in planning a session and then use the list to ensure you do not miss anything important out. You can focus on practical issues (room layouts, etc.; see **Practical preparation**), but you can also use checklists to audit content plan, as in example **54.1**, or plan your evaluation strategy.

At De Montfort University, The Information Source Evaluation Matrix (Towlson, Leigh and Mathers, 2009) (see example **62.1**) is a self-assessment tool or checklist used by learners to evaluate resources.

✓ BEST FOR

- Any training event, especially new or important events.
- Most learning contexts, especially encouraging independent learning and the development of critical thinking.

+ MORE

- Other ways of using checklists with learners include the provision of more interactive guidance with referencing, in devising prompts for peer or self-assessment (turning the learning outcomes into easily understandable assessment criteria) or in providing structured handouts for a literature search and review.
- As indicated above, checklists are used in many clinical settings

62.1

	1	2	3	4	5	Mark
Who? – is the author	Author background is unknown	Some evidence author works in this area but few articles available	Evidence of some publications in this area by author	Author has several published works in this area	Author is a known authority in this area	
Score						
What? – is the relevance of points made	Content and arguments of little or no relevance to the task	Only of peripheral/ little relevance to task being undertaken	Some of the content is relevant to task requirements	Several points made are of relevance to the task	Content and arguments closely match your needs	
Score						
Where? – context for points made	Situation to which author applies points is different to that of the task	Minimal similarity between author's context and the task context	Author's situation and that of the task have some similarity	Reasonable similarity between author's and task context	Author's context and that of the task very similar	
Score						
When? – was the source published	Date is unknown or older than 20 years old	Old reference: 10 to 20 years old	Reference is 5 to 10 years old	Recent reference: 2 to 5 years old	Up-to-date source: published in last 2 years	
Score						
Why? – author's reason/ purpose for writing the article	No apparent motivation seen in article	Newspaper (or online) article opinion – not evidenced	Trade magazine/ commercial paper – might have some bias	Book source/ conference paper or subject interest forum/blog	Academic journal paper – peer reviewed	
Score						
Source/ reference						
Total marks						

including evidence-based medicine (EBM). EBM starts from the premise that using and applying the results of health sciences research can improve medical practice. It draws on a range of techniques and approaches, including the use of randomized controlled trials, risk-benefit analysis, meta-analysis and systematic review of the literature. Key to systematic review is critical appraisal. This is 'the process of carefully and systematically examining research to judge its trustworthiness, and its value and relevance in a particular context' (Burls, 2009). A number of different critical appraisal training courses are available to develop the necessary skills to review the validity, results and relevance of scientific research.

- As discussed in Webb and Powis (2004), critical appraisal rests on an established framework, which defines the main learning outcomes and methodology underpinning the approach. Validated checklists of question prompts (or 'review appraisal tools') are provided by a number of sites, including the Centre for Evidence-Based Medicine (www.cebm.net/index.aspx?o=1913). The Critical Appraisal Skills Programme (CASP) (PHRU, 2007), though its funding has concluded, has some very well designed checklists that could be used in a range of sessions, not just applied to evidence-based practice (EBP) settings, and they certainly provide inspiration for how you might approach using checklists to structure a learning activity.
- Checklists can be used as the basis for individual work or to structure group discussions and feedback.

⁞ WATCH OUT

- When using checklists in planning your own sessions, ensure you review them when you finish and note whether you missed out any elements.
- When using checklists with learners, be careful that you provide a clear and comprehensive introduction to how you want your learners to use the lists. It is probably more effective to use the checklists within a learning and teaching event rather than provide them as supplementary handouts at the end of a session, as more can be gained from your learners completing the activity rather than having something which might be helpful but in their eyes is untested.

•◆ REFERENCES

Burls, A. (2009) *What is Critical Appraisal?* 2nd edn, Hayward Medical Communications, www.medicine.ox.ac.uk/bandolier/painres/download/whatis/What_is_critical_appraisal.pdf.

Public Health Resource Unit (PHRU) (2007) *Appraisal Tools*, www.phru.nhs.uk/pages/phd/resources.htm.

Towlson, K. M., Leigh, M. and Mathers, L. (2009) The Information Source Evaluation Matrix: a quick, easy and transferable content evaluation tool, *SCONUL Focus*, **47**, 15–19.

Webb, J. and Powis, C. (2004) Case study 8: Information literacy through critical appraisal. In Webb, J. and Powis, C. , *Teaching Information Skills: theory and practice*, Facet Publishing, 99–101.

Acknowledgement

Many thanks to Kaye Towlson, Mike Leigh and Lucy Mathers for permission to use the Information Source Evaluation Matrix.

63 Design briefs

This activity works best if you have some time with a group. Split the learners into small groups and ask them to work on a design brief. For example, you could ask them to plan a perfect library to help them understand how your library works as a building, plan a mini catalogue for a collection to help them understand classification and metadata, prepare an introductory library guide or design library web pages to help them understand the range of online services that you provide. This can be an excellent induction activity for learners with whom you expect to have a longer-term relationship. Not only will it help them understand how libraries work (for example, comparing your actual library to the one that they design) but it will also help inform your planning – an informal feedback mechanism.

The briefs need to be clear and well defined for them to work. If it is for a library building you should specify which core services are required. A small collection would be better than 'the history books' for understanding classification and cataloguing. If you set a task where your learners are asked to produce some kind of guide or information material, specify the level of readership and provide access to your publication guidelines.

✓ BEST FOR

- A group that you have some time with or as a set assignment
- Learners in creative subjects: design briefs are a standard assessment form for students in art and design disciplines.

+ MORE

- Ask the learners to provide a design brief for an architect or web designer – what would they want in a library building or on a library website?

❗ WATCH OUT

- You will need to explain the rationale for this in detail to engage the learners with the greatest effect. It can be a really rewarding activity but it might not appear relevant to them at first as it requires more time to settle in and get used to the task.

→ FURTHER READING

Design Council, www.designcouncil.org.uk/resources-and-events/Business-and-public-sector/guides/finding-and-working-with-a-designer/writing-a-brief-and-getting-a-project-started.

64 Discussions

Teaching sessions are often restricted to 'talk, demo, do' and, of course, this is sometimes an appropriate plan. However, a discursive element is rarely allowed into our teaching. This may be to do with the material or it may be to do with letting go of full control but there are occasions when a discussion amongst the group could illuminate issues that you want to cover. For example, a discussion of how learners typically find material could help more than a prescriptive 'best way to search' talk from you. Discussions will naturally tap into the experiences and knowledge of the group and help you to form clear strategies to help them build on that base. Discussions also allow the possibility for reflection on practice, thus encouraging deeper learning.

Have clear parameters for the discussion and always stay in control. Do not allow participants to stray too far from the topic but be flexible enough to follow interesting routes through it. Have a set of key questions and/or interventions ready and be prepared to take some notes as the discussion happens so that you can provide a summary at the end.

✓ BEST FOR

- groups
- mature learner
- staff development.

✚ MORE

- This will almost certainly work best with learners that are either mature enough to be comfortable discussing issues, with groups that have been together for some time and/or with groups with whom you have built up a relationship. Always prepare – this is not an activity that you can easily perform without some rescue strategies in reserve – and have a summary of the main issues ready to act as prompts or instead of the discussion if it is failing.

- A discussion can be structured using a handout or guidance on a slide – this can help keep the discussion on track and to time. It will also help guide your learners to reach conclusions rather than just have a rambling discussion. You might want to have a handout that has a series of key questions to guide the discussion.
- Remember, you might be able to elicit some of these questions from the learners before the session – especially if this is a staff development event – so you make the discussion even more explicitly structured around the learners' needs and wants.
- Short discussions can enliven a lecture style presentation. (See **Buzz groups**.)

❉ WATCH OUT

- Do not let one or two individuals dominate the discussion. Be prepared to moderate the debate by asking those who are not contributing anything for their opinions but be careful to ask specific questions rather than for general observations – this makes it easier for more reluctant participants to contribute to the discussion.

65 Dividing the dots

This activity is an active way of enabling a group to express opinion and show preference for a given set of options. It gets your learners on their feet and gives them the opportunity to express their opinions relatively anonymously. It can be used for any situation where you want to be able to rank a range of options. For example, you could have a range of search terms or sources of information, and ask a group to decide which would be the best options.

The options need to be displayed on a wall with enough space next to each option for the group to stick their dots, so flip-chart paper is probably the best option. If you have a small group, sticky notes may be sufficient.

Give each person five sticky dots. Ask them to allocate the dots to the best option or options (for example, all five dots could go to one option or three to one and two to another, and so on.). Set a time limit for the activity – no more than five or ten minutes. Once the activity is finished you can count up the dots and review the findings.

✓ BEST FOR

- enabling individual contribution from a group
- adding activity to a teaching session
- making quick group decisions.

✚ MORE

- One of the strengths of this approach, as opposed to using voting systems, is that it enables learners to set priorities and rank between options rather than a yes/no answer. Participants have time to choose rather than feel rushed. It also allows plenty of opportunity for personal decision-making rather than learners anxiously looking at how their peers are voting. You can use the process as well as the outcomes as a focus for discussion.

- Ways of changing the process include dividing up the group so that not all the participants choose – some instead lobby for particular options.
- If you're short of dots, ask learners to use pens to draw dots – this does mean you'll have to trust them to only add the number of dots you've allowed them!

⁞ WATCH OUT

- Learners reluctant to participate may try to hang back or just try to divide all the dots evenly. Personal preference – over who has championed one option – may dominate the process with some groups who refuse to engage fully with the task.

66 Drawing the line

This activity is ideal for provoking discussion related to the complex ethical issues related to using information. The example in **66.1** focuses on plagiarism.

One of the main problems of dealing with plagiarism is a lack of awareness of what it actually constitutes. This activity includes several examples of behaviour that may or may not be plagiarism, starting with an example that definitely *is* plagiarism and finishing with an example that definitely *is not* plagiarism. Your learners must draw the line between the remaining behaviours and decide where to draw the line between acceptable and unacceptable behaviour.

Break your learners into groups of around 4–6 people. Allow 15–20 minutes for discussion and then run a feedback session. The line should be drawn between numbers 4 and 5, but you may find your learners disagree!

....

66.1

....

In the list below, item 1 is plagiarism and item 6 is not. In your group, decide where you would draw the line in the list between what *is* and *is not* plagiarism.

1. Copying a paragraph verbatim from a source without any acknowledgement.
2. Copying a paragraph and making small changes, e.g. replacing a few verbs or adjectives with synonyms. Source is included in the list of references.
3 Cutting and pasting a paragraph by using sentences of the original work but omitting one or two and putting one or two in a different order; no quotation marks used. Including an acknowledgement in the text, e.g. (Jones, 1999) plus inclusion in the reference list.
4. Composing a paragraph by taking short phrases of 10 to 15 words from a number of sources and putting them together, adding words of your own to make a coherent whole. All sources are included in reference list.
5. Paraphrasing a paragraph with substantial changes in language and organization; the new version also has changes in the amount of detail used and the examples cited. Acknowledgement included in the text, e.g. (Jones, 1999), and in the reference list.

6. Quoting a paragraph by placing it in block format with the source cited in the text and in the list of references.

✓ BEST FOR

- Highlighting understanding (or lack thereof) of a specific topic. This task is especially effective for plagiarism and good academic practice.
- Provoking discussion.

✚ MORE

- This activity could be used with staff and students, in groups or on an individual basis. It can be adapted to any suitable topic by replacing the examples. For example, referencing styles, copyright (e.g. use of images or music).
- Rather than have a sliding scale of examples, this exercise could be simplified to the discussion of standalone examples. See the JISC Netskills (n.d.) website for examples.

❗ WATCH OUT

- Make sure your examples and the context for the session are relevant to your learners. For example, do not just use a familiar set of generic examples for references, but try to use examples in subject areas relevant to the specific groups of learners with whom you will be working. Examples from history texts would work well with history students, but not those studying textiles or business studies.

➥ REFERENCES

This task is based on an exercise in Swales, J. and Feak, C. (1994) *Academic Writing for Graduate Students*, University of Michigan. Also featured in Carroll, J. (2002) *A Handbook for Deterring Plagiarism in Higher Education*, Oxford Centre for Staff Development.

JISC Netskills (n.d.) *Plagiarism Materials for Secondary Schools*, www.netskills.ac.uk/content/projects/eduserv-info-lit/plagiarism-materials.html.

Acknowledgement

Many thanks to Jude Carroll, Oxford Centre for Staff Development and University of Michigan Press, for permission to reproduce this activity.

67 Fear cards

Give all participants a small card or piece of paper and ask them to write down the thing that they fear most about finding information, referencing or whatever you are teaching. Collect the cards, collate, and address in the session.

This can give you valuable insight into what the learners already know (their fears will stem from this) and also what you should prioritize. There is little point in ploughing ahead with your session if the learners are blocked by something that you may not have planned to cover.

This approach is a less challenging way of eliciting honest responses from participants who might not want to share their concerns out loud with their peers.

✓ BEST FOR
- anyone
- tailoring sessions to group needs.

✚ MORE
- Fear cards could be used in pairs or small groups, starting as the basis for a discussion. For more confident groups you could ask them to brainstorm their fears.
- This could also work as a pre-session audit, asking for the same information via a VLE, e-mail survey, or sudents' tutors. This approach also gives you the option of responding individually to the learners after the session via e-mail or the VLE.

⁚ WATCH OUT
- There are two risks with this approach. The first is that participants give silly or flippant responses. Secondly, you could also open up topics that

will hijack your session – these might be personal or institutional issues – over which you have no control. In the latter case, you would need to acknowledge these, but explain clearly that the scope of your session means these issues cannot be addressed.

- Using fear cards at the start of a session requires confidence to deal with the unexpected and the ability to adapt to the respondents' fears – there is no point in using the activity if the information is not used. If you do not feel up to this, then collect in the cards (or gather your information) prior to the session. This allows you time to prepare and adapt your session.

68 Future scenarios

The use of scenarios in teaching, through case studies, for example, is common. This activity involves using scenarios from the future, and imagining worlds that may or may never exist. This technique is based on scenario planning, a method used by many businesses and organizations to plan for unexpected events. However, as full scenario planning is a complex and time-consuming process, this activity simply borrows some of the imaginative methods used. See example **68.1**.

68.1 *A day in the life*

This activity involves learners imagining a future world where a particular situation that you would like to explore exists. A world 20 years from now is a good margin as it allows enough time for the world to be significantly different from our own. Examples that could be interesting to explore for information skills teaching include: a world where Google controls all channels of communication or where there are no copyright restrictions.

Describe the world to your learners, being as creative and engaging as you can. Instead of simply describing the future world, talk as if you already live there. You could use music, images and newspaper headlines to help you make the world real. Try to talk generally about the world, as your learners will be asked to flesh out the details in their activity.

Ask your learners to imagine a day in the life of a particular character, such as a student or an academic. Get your learners to draw out details for this character and imagine how they live (for example, what do they wear? How do they travel? Which technologies are used? What are the popular interests?). Ask your learners to be as imaginative as they like and draw pictures. As well as general questions about your character's life, you will need to provide focused questions for the particular issue you wish them to consider – for example, how are libraries used (do libraries even exist?)? How do people access information?

✓ BEST FOR

- exploring the implications of a trend (such as copyright, plagiarism or reliance on Google) and developing critical thinking, thus drawing out a debate
- engaging learners.

✚ MORE

- If you have more time, ask the learners to frame their own future scenarios, rather than working with a framework which you have set.
- Use an existing scenario as the basis of your activities (see Neville Freeman (2009), www.futurelibraries.info/content and JISC infoNet's Scenario Planning infoKit, www.jiscinfonet.ac.uk/tools/scenario-planning for further reading and links to existing scenarios).

❗ WATCH OUT

- You need to set the ground rules very carefully for this session, establishing the basis for the future scenario-planning activity – it is important that learners don't question the scenario; they have to simply go with it and imagine how life would be. You must also be committed to the activity as any hesitance or reluctance on your part will amplify any possible resistance from participants.
- If you do not feel comfortable leading this activity (perhaps some of the content was designed by others), do not go ahead – if you do not feel enthusiastic you will undermine the real virtues of the task. If you *are* enthusiastic about it, it will work very well: learners love opportunities to develop their imagination and share their plans.

⇢ REFERENCE

Neville Freeman Agency (2009) *The Bookends Scenarios: alternative futures for the public library network in NSW in 2030*, Library Council, www.sl.nsw.gov.au/services/public_libraries/publications/docs/bookendsscenarios.pdf.

69 Games

Introducing an element of competition into your sessions may be a useful way to engage learners with information skills. It will be unexpected and can add colour and variety to the session for you as well as for the learners.

There are many examples of games that you could use but probably the most effective approach is to adapt a familiar format. Examples include:

- The pub quiz: put the learners into small groups and have different rounds of questions/tasks with prizes for each round and for the overall winning team. (See **Pub quizzes**.)
- The game show: replicate panel games by creating teams who have to complete tasks or solve puzzles.
- Treasure hunts: these are particularly effective with younger learners who could be asked to solve clues around the library or learning centre to find the main prize.
- Online games: although an effective 'shoot 'em up' for an information literacy topic may be tricky, the typical online or video game involves solving a series of puzzles and collecting items (information) that lead to a prize. The game equates to trying to find information to complete an assignment.
- Introducing an element of game play to a simple task: the University of Northampton's Liberation Referencing Tutorial is a straight grab-and-move exercise to arrange the elements of a reference in the correct order. The game comes with the introduction of a cartoon cat (Harvey) who suffers if the answer is wrong or is rewarded if the answer is correct (see picture **69.1**).

69.1 *Harvey the cat when well, when put on strict rations and after getting in a fight. Reproduced by kind permission of Georgina Payne, University of Northampton.*

The same rules apply to games as to any other activity with which you ask learners to engage. The learners should be able to see how the game links to the learning outcomes for the session and what the benefits of active participation are. The latter could and should include some fun but this should not be the only rationale!

✓ BEST FOR

Depends on the game, this activity is particularly effective for:

- younger learners
- jaded teachers
- those expecting a boring and passive session.

+ MORE

- The best advice is to get it right before you use it – this is especially true of online games. The video-game industry spends millions on getting games right, and your learners will expect similar levels of sophistication from you. Simple can be good but looking amateurish is not. Test your online games extensively before you release them and make sure to use testers who will be frank with you.

? WATCH OUT

- Some learners will not engage with the game. Be sensitive but firm – it is just as much a learning activity as is more formal group work.

→ FURTHER READING

Clyde, J. and Thomas, C. (2008) Building an Information Literacy First Person Shooter, *Reference Services Review*, **36** (4), 366–80.

Library Games (2006) *Information Literacy Game*, http://librarygames.blogspot.com/2006/10/information-literacy-game.html.

Manhattenville College Library (n.d.) *Libraries, Literacy and Gaming*, http://mville.libguides.com/content.php?pid=44589&sid=331099.

70 Goldfish bowl

This activity is ideal for any topic that involves debate such as issues relating to copyright, plagiarism, authority, privacy online or managing your online reputation. Arrange chairs in a circle, placing two in the centre. Two volunteers should sit in the central chairs and begin the debate: they are in the centre of the 'goldfish bowl', being observed by the wider group. If a member of the wider group wants to join the debate, challenge one of the speakers or have their own say, they must tap one of the learners in the middle on the shoulder, and then wait their turn.

✓ BEST FOR

- confident learners
- providing a novel approach to managing discussion in a large group
- enabling participants to see how to structure a debate
- energizing discussion by involving movement
- providing an effective compromise between involving the whole group in a learning activity, and having something managed and focused.

✚ MORE

- As preparation for the goldfish bowl, divide the class into small discussion groups and give each group one side of the debate to research and discuss. This will mean learners have a chance to consider the issues relating to the debate and encourage learners to be more confident in their contributions. The preparation could take place immediately prior to the goldfish bowl, or set as homework.
- Break up a large group into two or more simultaneous goldfish bowls – this might be less daunting to participants and thus encourage participation.
- Some example topics for discussion:
  - Is it OK to download music illegally?

— What is wrong with copying and pasting for my class work?
— Privacy online: Google and Facebook retain a lot of your personal information – is this good or bad?

: WATCH OUT

- This activity requires a motivated group of learners in order to work well. The choice of topic is vital as it must be one that engages the group and thus provoke discussion.
- Keep an eye out for the discussion being dominated by a few members of the group. You may have to encourage quieter learners to contribute.
- If the discussion stalls, be prepared to join in yourself with some controversial or thought-provoking comments or questions.

71 Guided tours

A guided tour can be the most effective way of introducing your library or information service to a new user. It can also be mind-numbingly boring and pointless, reinforcing all the negative stereotypes of librarians. Plan it carefully!

Good guided tours enable the learners to understand how and why to use a library and information service, and most importantly, the tour will help them to visualize how they will do this for themselves. Try to start from the standpoint of the learner, and find out a little bit about them. Have they ever used this library before? Have they been into the building on a campus tour (in the case of students)? What is their programme of study? Have they used libraries much?

It can be helpful to see the guided tour as a story about how your learners will encounter the service. Remember that the mechanics of how to find and borrow a book, log on to computers, and print or photocopy will be important to them, especially as many of the procedures will be specific to your own library. The users will also want to get a sense of where their resources are and how the different kinds of space are used. Libraries are often overwhelming places to new users, and you need to break down your learners' barriers and help them make the most of the services and resources available.

If possible, find ways of making the session interactive. Take a library card so you can demonstrate how to borrow a book, get members of the group to search the library catalogue, and set someone a task to find a book on the shelf.

Think very carefully about the tone you adopt and the language you use. Library jargon should always be explained if its use is unavoidable. Use clear and simple sentences, and try to personalize it if appropriate. Do not avoid the difficult questions – 'Yes, you will need to buy *some* books' – but focus always on the positive. Remember, libraries are focal points for learning, and they change lives and opportunities. You are an advocate for the wonder of all libraries.

✓ BEST FOR

- small groups.

✦ MORE

- Tailor the tour to be relevant to the learners you are with and focus on how they will actually use the library. Do not worry about giving them every little detail if it is not relevant.

❗ WATCH OUT

- For stragglers: if the group is too large, the tour will inevitably stretch out. Try to gather everyone together at critical points on the tour. Engage the others in conversation while you wait for the tail-enders to catch up.

72 Hands-on workshops

Workshops are probably the most common form of information skills teaching and this is unsurprising given the essentially practical nature of the subject. Information literacy combines the application of theory to the practical business of locating, analysing and using information. Information skills can be fairly dull to the average, pragmatic learner who wants to get the information for an entirely different reason than to become 'information literate'. All this means that the sooner that you allow your learners to get some hands-on work the better – workshops provide this opportunity.

Typically, a workshop will consist of a short introductory talk, a demonstration and learners working on problems either set by the teacher or stemming from their immediate needs. This model is not a bad one, although it can encourage laziness in planning. The hands-on element is probably the area least prepared for. All the time in planning is spent on preparing the introductory slides, working out a good demonstration and then simply leaving the learners to get on with the hands-on section – searching for something that they are interested in or following a series of mechanistic steps outlined in a handout or quiz sheet. However, the hands-on element should be the part where the learners really start to process any learning through active practice of theory.

The obvious application of hands-on activity is with a computer. For example, if you have a group confident in using the web, delaying the hands-on activity will only frustrate them – give them something to do immediately and then bring them back for a demonstration or some theory. For example, you might ask them to find something on a topic at the beginning of the session. Look at what they have found and use it to audit where they are with their search skills, and also use it as a basis to talk about improving or changing the searches. This has the side effect of instilling confidence that the learners can find something or in gently showing the over-confident that they have something to learn. Starting a workshop in this way provides a basis that you can build on in a much more collaborative way than if you were simply telling the learners what to do.

✓ BEST FOR

- all practical elements of information skills.

✚ MORE

- Make your workshops interactive: allow learners the chance to work with material and to ask questions of their peers and teacher.
- Ensure the workshop forms part of a framework: give the learners some idea of why they are working like this and what they are working towards.
- Include activities for the learners to take away, thus providing further opportunities to put their skills into practice.
- Incorporate some form of assessment: this can be a simple worksheet, peer or self-assessment or involve formative feedback from the teacher. The learners should have some idea whether they are progressing through the workshop in the right direction.
- Have a goal: this can be wide-ranging and loose but it should be expressed clearly. Learners may not immediately see the point of the things you are asking them to do so make it explicit what they should achieve – this can be something set by you or can come from their own immediate or long-term aims.
- Try using peer support to help the less able or less confident learners with their hands-on work.

❗ WATCH OUT

- Allow enough time for the hands-on activity – this should be at the heart of a workshop so aim for twice as much activity as your direct input.
- Always make sure that any exercise you set for the hands-on element of a session has a point. Aimlessly completing quiz sheets that do not directly relate to the learners' needs will not be met with enthusiasm and thus any learning will probably be lost.
- Be careful to ensure that the practical element of a workshop is allowed to dominate – it should not be an excuse for a lecture. You do not necessarily need to be in a computer lab to run a workshop. Use group discussion, poster tours and other collaborative exercises as an alternative.

73 Ice-breakers

Ice-breakers are activities used at the start of a teaching session or course to 'warm up' the group so they will feel more relaxed and comfortable with each other. Ice-breakers can serve many purposes, but are particularly important if your teaching session involves group work.

Many training courses often start with an ice-breaker focused on individual introductions, but ice-breakers can also be main activities, which may often be more suitable to information skills sessions where there may not always be time to run formal introductions.

The purpose of an ice-breaker is to break down barriers between individuals within the teaching group in order to encourage them to be more participative and engaged in the activities. This can be particularly useful whether the group members are strangers or colleagues who may feel inhibited by status or role.

One example of an introductory ice-breaker would be to break your learners into pairs and ask each learner to find out three facts about their partner – this could be routine information such as their job or course, or something a little more unusual, such as the job they wanted to have when they were a child. Each learner must then introduce their partner to the rest of the group. Be careful with this technique if you are using it to gather information to guide the content of your session – what is reported may not necessarily be accurate! Consider giving learners the chance to comment on their partner's introduction.

✓ BEST FOR

- group work
- breaking down barriers at the start of sessions
- creating an active environment for learning.

+ MORE

- If you have a large number of learners, run ice-breakers in small groups rather than for the group as a whole. It is better for some of your learners to have bonded than none at all.

- Consider using your ice-breaker as a way of gathering information to help you guide the session.
- An activity-style ice-breaker could be:
  — something fun and totally unrelated to the session you are running
  — a fun activity that can provide some 'lessons learned' to feed into your session
  — a group or paired learning activity which forms part of your aims and objectives for the session – if time is short, simply starting with an activity rather than a presentation can act as an ice-breaker.

⁑ WATCH OUT

- Introductory ice-breakers usually involve divulging some personal information – ensure what you ask is not too sensitive.
- Younger learners may respond better to an activity-style ice-breaker rather than an introductory ice-breaker.
- Some ice-breakers can seem like a forced activity – make sure you are enthusiastic about yours.

74 Interviewing

Interviewing can be used as an activity to involve learners in researching a particular subject matter, as well as giving the opportunity to practice questioning and listening skills. The interviewing technique can be used as a method of simply sharing information or as a basis for discussion within a larger group.

Interviewing can work well in a variety of contexts. It can be a very helpful approach in a simulation – where you are asking participants to weigh up evidence for a research task, such as a fictional trial of King Richard III. It can also work effectively with other groups of learners in quite different situations. For example, interviewing can work very well as a way of eliciting personal experiences of information literacy behaviours from a member of your group, or perhaps exploring an issue with an invited speaker.

Interviewing activities could be elaborated to involve an element of role play, where learners are asked to research a part and then play a journalist or television interviewer. It can be fun to put historical characters into a modern-day context, such as Henry VIII and his wives on a Jerry Springer-style show.

✓ BEST FOR

- developing listening and questioning skills
- social learning.

✚ MORE

- Interviewing could easily be altered to a courtroom setting, where learners play witnesses, defendants and prosecutors. This activity could potentially get complicated if played out as a 'real' trial, so asking the 'witnesses' and 'defendants' to give statements, and allowing the opportunity for questions, could simplify it. The whole group can act as a judge at the end, with an ensuing discussion. The trial could be used as a vehicle for testing accuracy of information and bias, and asking learners to make a decision on the information provided. You could even put information sources on trial, with learners defending and prosecuting, for example, Google or Wikipedia.

- When using interviewing as a method of practicing questioning and listening skills, learners can work in groups of three. One person interviews, one is the interviewee and the third person observes and provides feedback on techniques used.
- Ask an invited speaker to be interviewed by your learners. For example, if you are running a session on literature searching, compiling literature reviews or the use of bibliographic software, you could ask someone who has previously completed this task to talk to – or rather be interviewed by – current learners.

❖ WATCH OUT

- Many learners are reluctant to take part in role play, and some may find this type of activity awkward, so you will need to use techniques to put them at their ease. Ice-breaker activities could help, but also allowing the interviews to take place in small groups or on a one-to-one basis (and reporting back) may be less daunting.

75 Jigsaws

Jigsaw activities are where learners, individually or in groups, are given a number of tasks that together will create something. Typically, this is about finding individual pieces of information that will build up into a solution to a problem. Individuals or groups work in isolation and then try to match their piece of information with the most appropriate, and so on, until the whole is identified.

This approach has an interesting focus on both the individual elements and the task as a whole. It can be a very effective way of enabling learners to see the different stages or components of a research task, and also how a conclusion is achieved collaboratively.

It could be combined with gaming in a murder mystery style (solve a mystery by locating and solving clues around the library) or with a treasure map exercise as part of an induction to the library. Ask learners to put together a guide by identifying key pieces of information, or find a number of resources for a learning pack, and so on, instead of taking them on a traditional tour.

✓ BEST FOR

- all levels of learner, but especially good with younger learners.

+ MORE

- With a slightly different brief, it could be divided into a 'The Apprentice'-style research task, with the whole picture only revealed through collaboration at the end.
- This works best as a group exercise. Allow collaboration so a group that has found its 'piece' of the jigsaw can help out other groups who have yet to succeed with their task.
- This type of activity can work well as an ice-breaker – learners have to interact with each other to solve the puzzle.

‽ WATCH OUT

- This can fail if one of the groups does not engage or otherwise fails to find their piece of the jigsaw. Be prepared to step in if this is the case and provide help and encouragement.

76 Lectures

Lectures often get a bad press – they conjure up images of rows of bored faces, someone dozing in a corner of the lecture theatre, droning teachers, and poorly written presentations. But, if the topic and presentation are right, a lecture can be an inspiring and motivating event.

You are most likely to get involved as a way of dealing with a particularly large group and although this is not a valid pedagogical reason for lecturing over any other activity, it is practical. Whatever the reason behind the lecture, you should:

- Plan the inputs and activities in the same way as for a workshop or practical. Do not assume that you will be speaking all the time.
- Check your slides or presentation and look at them as if you are a learner. Are they readable from the back, do they have too many distractions (e.g. animations), are they dull?
- Check that your voice projects to the back of the room or wear a microphone.
- Include some audience participation by asking learners to work with their neighbour on something or turn around to discuss a point (see **Buzz groups**). Try to break up your speaking every ten minutes or so. You could include short films, audio files, pictures – anything to maintain attentiveness.
- Try team teaching – a change of voice is always welcome.

✓ BEST FOR

- large groups
- providing a framework.

+ MORE

- Learners will probably expect a lecture to be passive so work in some hands-on activity. (See **Buzz groups, Demonstrations, Presentations, Cephalonian method, Building blocks** for other ways to improve a lecture.)

❗ WATCH OUT

- Lectures can cause anxiety in a teacher – try to remember that the learners are all individuals, and try to speak to one or two of them rather than the whole room. If you build in interactivity, remember that you also need to be able to assert your authority when you want that activity to stop.

77 Mind maps

A mind map is a visual, non-linear method of noting information. Mind maps usually follow a tree-like structure, with branches coming off a central topic. There is no set way to mind map – it can be as creative as the individual learner prefers, using colours, symbols and images if so desired (see examples **77.1** and **77.2**). Tony Buzan, often cited as the inventor of mind maps, recommends making your mind map as colourful and visually appealing as possible, even preferring curved lines to straight, in order to stimulate the brain. Mind maps can be used to help learners visualize search problems and think through the search process, identifying concepts and keywords. Mind maps have been shown to improve students' searching, with students making the link between the mind map and the search process (Webber, 2002).

A concept map is similar to a mind map, but in addition contains lines that show the relationships between the concepts displayed within the map. This can be used to help plan search strategies, indicating how different concepts should be connected (AND, OR, NOT).

There are many computer programs (e.g. MindGenius, www.mindgenius. com; iMind map, www.thinkbuzan.com) and websites (e.g. bubbl.us, http://bubbl.us; Mindomo, www.mindomo.com) that will help you create mind maps. However, pen and paper is often the most preferred method!

Provide each learner with a large blank piece of paper and some coloured marker pens. Ask your learners to create a mind map of the topic they wish to research. The main subject should be placed in the centre of the paper. Sub-topics are the 'branches'. Ask them to note any information they like. Encourage the use of colours and images – learners should make this map their own.

Once learners have completed their maps, explain how this can then be used to select keywords, identify search concepts and combine keywords. For example, ask learners to link which words should be combined with AND/OR and which words they might want to exclude using NOT. Ask students to mark which words they used in their searches. The mind map can then be used as a reference for learners to return to when researching the topic.

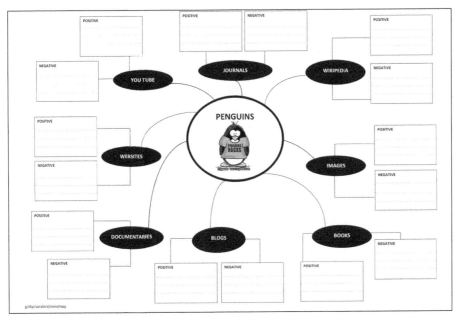

77.1 *A scaffolded mind map where students fill in appropriate information. Created by Sara Bird at Newcastle University Library and used with partner schools visiting the library (reproduced with permission).*

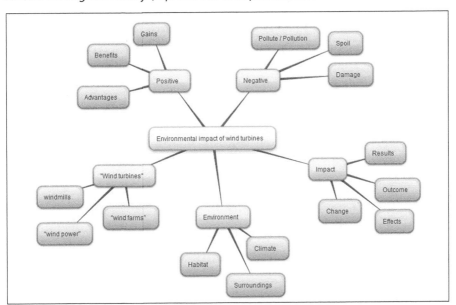

77.2 *An example of a mind map to be used to develop search concepts and generate keywords (created using bubbl.us, a free online mind-mapping tool, http://bubbl.us)*

✓ BEST FOR

- visual learners
- brainstorming and note taking
- planning search strategies
- defining search concepts and identifying keywords
- mapping existing knowledge of a topic and identifying gaps
- providing evidence of the learning process.

✚ MORE

- Ask learners to mind map their knowledge and perceptions of a subject both before and after carrying out research. This can be used to aid reflection on learning and search strategies.
- Mind maps can be used for note taking. To practice mind-mapping skills, ask learners to watch a video or presentation and note the key points using a mind map. Have a 'gallery' of maps afterwards to compare what learners thought were the key points.
- When learners are mapping the same topic, it can be interesting to compare mind maps in order to compare different approaches to a topic.
- Webber (2002) suggests the following uses for mind maps:
  - Helping students to visualize their view of a search problem.
  - Creating a reference point for potential search terms.
  - Providing a reference point for the success of the search.
  - Obliging students to spend more time planning the search, and encouraging them to think of the process.

❗ WATCH OUT

- Mind maps do not suit the learning style of some people. They may prefer using other methods and so may need more support in creating mind maps.

➻ REFERENCE

Webber, S. (2002) Mapping a Path to the Empowered Searcher. In Graham, C. (ed.) *Online Information 2002: Proceedings: 3–5 December 2002, Learned Information Europe*, 177–181, http://dis.sheffield.ac.uk/sheila/sw-mind map-2002.pdf.

Acknowledgment

Many thanks to Sara Bird at Newcastle University for permission to include her mind map.

78 Multiple-choice questions

Multiple-choice is a form of assessment in which respondents are asked to select the best (or correct) choice (or choices) from a list of options. Such questions are used very often in educational settings, but also in market research and in popular quiz formats. You may encounter them most often in technology-enhanced learning (TEL). Many VLEs have integrated quiz and survey software and hand-held voting (or personal response) systems are very suited to interactive learning activities in the form of multiple-choice responses.

There are always two different parts to a multiple-choice question. The first is the 'stem' – a question, an incomplete statement or a problem to be solved. The second part is the list of possible answers – the 'key'. Incorrect answers are called 'distractors'.

You can use lots of different formats for the stem – images, case studies or single-line statements. There are some important principles to follow when developing your questions (University of Leeds, 2006):

- Think very carefully about your use of language. Try to prepare clear, succinct and unambiguous stems.
- Avoid repeating content in the options.
- Usually it is best just to have one correct response.
- Make sure that you do not have silly, implausible options. It may be better to think about what are most likely to be the misunderstandings of your learners.
- Base your questions on topics that have been covered by the session. Assessing things that haven't been taught breaks one of the golden rules of assessment – that it should be fair.
- Think about whether you want to provide your learners with the opportunity to re-take the test. Some learners are motivated by taking tests again to improve their performance.
- Don't give the answer away!
- Make the questions challenging – two obviously wrong answers and one

clearly right will not encourage learning.

- Don't encourage guessing – if the answers are too complicated or impenetrable, then learners will simply attempt to guess them.
- Preferably, give answers immediately after the choice has been taken – answers should include some feedback/explanation as well as the simple right/wrong choice.
- Test the questions if you can – would random choices of answers get high marks? Vary where the right answer is.

Some sample multiple-choice questions used in assessments at De Montfort University are shown in example **78.1**. These questions are used within an online assessment for part of a compulsory module on first year pharmacy courses. All learning materials are available through the VLE. The teaching comprises a series of workshops with a concluding mandatory assessment. All the questions are linked very closely to module learning materials and the specified learning outcomes. See **Checklists** for more information on the Information Source Evaluation Matrix.

....
78.1
....

1. Evaluating information sources

    It is important to evaluate the reliability and validity of the information sources that you use in your academic work. De Montfort Library Services' Information Source Evaluation Matrix provides a useful framework for assessing different types of information.

    Use the criteria outlined by the Information Source Evaluation Matrix to answer this question:

    Which of the following five factors is the strongest indicator that a book or journal article's author is an expert in their chosen field, and therefore a reliable source of information?

    a. Author is a known authority in their chosen field, and has written books and articles in professional publications.
    b. Author has several published works within their chosen field.
    c. Evidence of some publications within a specific field by an author.
    d. Some evidence that an author works in a professional capacity within a specific field but has few published articles.
    e. Author's background is unknown.

2. Evaluating information sources

It is important to evaluate the reliability and validity of the information sources that you use in your academic work. De Montfort Library Services' Information Source Evaluation Matrix provides a useful framework for assessing different types of information.

Using the criteria outlined by the Information Source Evaluation Matrix, what would be a strong indicator that the information in a book or journal article is current and up to date?

a. The information has been published in the last 2 years.

b. The information is 2 to 5 years old.

c. The information is 5 to 10 years old.

d. The information is 10 to 20 years old.

e. The information is 20-plus years old or has no identifiable date.

3. Plagiarism

Plagiarism is defined by University Student Regulations as: 'The significant use by a student of other people's work and the submission of it as though it were his or her own.'

Within an assignment, which one or more of the following actions would you consider as constituting plagiarism?

a. Deliberately attempting to gain advantage by presenting an individual or organization's work as if it were your own.

b. Substantially duplicating another individual or organization's work without acknowledging the original source.

c. Including a full list of all references used and studied in a bibliography at the end of your assignment.

d. Acknowledging your sources by citing correctly each source that you have used within your assignment text.

4. Referencing

Based on the materials used during the taught sessions, and using information taken from De Montfort University Student Regulations, which one or more of the following statements is correct?

'When writing your assignments it is important to reference all sources that you have used in your academic work, including

a. direct quotations taken from books, journals and the internet.

b. ideas and information taken from books, journals and the internet, which you used and have re-phrased.'

Answers:

You must acknowledge the origin of both direct quotations and ideas and information taken from other sources within your assignments.

✓ BEST FOR

- providing a quick assessment tool
- online learning and technology-enabled learning spaces.

✚ MORE

- Make a game of it by basing advancement or achievement in the game through correctly answering the questions. The consequence of a choice could be illustrated by committing the learner to a particular path based on each choice.

❢ WATCH OUT

- Too many multiple-choice exercises can be boring or pitched at the wrong level. Vary multiple-choice with other types of simple question (such as click-and-drag or missing-word exercises).

➼ REFERENCES

University of Leeds (2006) *Tips for Designing Multiple-Choice Questions*, Staff and Departmental Development Unit, www.sddu.leeds.ac.uk/online_resources/assessment/objective/good_questions.htm.

Acknowledgement

Many thanks to Paul Cavanagh, Department of Library Services, De Montfort University for supplying the sample questions.

79 Peer assessment

Peer assessment involves learners in the assessment of the work of their peers, i.e. other learners. It is a very powerful and effective approach to assessment, as hearing the views of peers on your performance and/or giving your considered opinion on their work can encourage engagement with both the tasks and the assessment process (knowing your peers will be judging you is an excellent motivator).

Involving learners in the assessment – that is, checking whether the learning outcomes have been achieved – can improve an understanding of both the task and the assessment process. It can also be a good way of validating your session content and design by getting the learners to take more responsibility for their learning outcomes. With information literacy teaching this may be especially important in translating what may seem like quite abstract (and library-owned) knowledge into meaningful and relevant applications. Most of the assessment will be formative and will take place within the session.

These are two of the ways you can use peer assessment:

1 Set a task and then ask for feedback on how the individual or group performed. Rather than you as teacher commenting on the feedback or results of the task, get the group to review their performance within the group.
2 Ask one group to comment and provide feedback to another group. For this to work effectively, the learners need to understand the assessment criteria which in turn should be based on the learning outcomes. Thus, if you ask for comments on a search strategy presented by a group, then you should require the peer assessors to comment specifically on particular elements – the range of keywords, perhaps – rather than general comments. This will require you to 'publish' the assessment criteria – a simple sheet of things to look for will suffice. Turn this into a more active group activity with a poster tour (**Poster tours**). This can work very well in assessing presentations.

✓ BEST FOR

- longer sessions
- staff development.

✚ MORE

- Try this as an online activity by using the comments facility in blogs, wikis or online discussion fora in other online learning environments. Make sure the assessment is anonymous to avoid any destructive comments.

❗ WATCH OUT

- Peer assessment can take a little while to introduce, so it is best used within longer sessions (or a series of classes) and with groups or individuals that are comfortable with each other.
- This activity requires trust and engagement. Some learners may lack the maturity to engage fully, simply be uncomfortable with what seems a strange approach, and will be destructive or, more likely, turn it into a joke. Others may not wish to comment for fear of receiving negative feedback when it is their turn or simply not want to challenge the status of more dominant learners by criticizing them. Exercises like the poster tours or online versions of peer assessment will allow anonymous feedback, thus possibly encouraging more active involvement from participants.
- Learners may also see this as an opt-out of the teacher's responsibility. Assessment and feedback, some will believe, is the role of the teacher, not of their peers. You will need to be clear in framing the peer-assessment activity by, for example, being very apparent about the assessment criteria and by providing helpful feedback prompts.

→ FURTHER READING

Hinett, K. and Thomas, J. (1999) *Staff Guide to Self and Peer Assessment*, Oxford Centre for Staff and Learning Development.

80 Podcasts

Podcasts are often confused with sound bites. The former are part of a series and the latter are one-off recordings. Both are downloadable sound files that can be listened to immediately or saved for later consumption. They are particularly useful for self-guided inductions to your service or as a series of skills tutorials that build into a course. Typically, they are loaded onto a web page or put within a VLE.

Ideally, podcasts should be short in order to control file length and manage boredom on the listener's part. Plan your podcast by defining its structure and give timings for each item. Decide how you will move from one item to the next. Plan any extra resources you may need, such as adding background music.

Test the voice used on people before committing to the series – it is often better to use more than one voice (in a double act) to maintain interest. The presenters should always introduce themselves and say what the podcast is about. Write a short storyboard for your podcast, but not a word-for-word script – otherwise it may sound stilted, artificial and forced. Instead, run through the things that you want the presenter to say and ask him or her to speak as if to one person rather than an audience. Often, 'amateur' voices from within the workplace are used and, although these can often work very well, speaking on a broadcast is a skill and not everyone can do it. Be ruthless when choosing your presenters.

Some topics lend themselves well to this format. For example: the self-guided tour asking learners to stop at pre-arranged points, short introductions to services like interlibrary loans or a series on referencing (how to reference a book and a journal, etc.).

✓ BEST FOR

- distance learners
- inductions.

✚ MORE

- Include some pictures – a video or stills of relevant views – and create a vodcast (video podcast) for a library tour.
- Use a more personal approach by interviewing library staff, lecturers/teachers and learners, asking them to outline their strategies for success in finding and using information.
- An interview with an author or a magazine-style podcast with book reviews may be more appropriate in other library settings to promote reading.
- Use podcasts to create digests of teaching sessions and upload it to your VLE or other online fora. These can be especially useful to help with revision or frequently asked questions.

❣ WATCH OUT

- Be wary of your listeners' attention span. Keep your audio files short – between two and two-and-a-half minutes is long enough. If you need to spend longer, split the files up and create a series.
- File formats can be a problem. Test the files in a number of formats – do they play in all of the machines that your users are likely to have?

81 Portfolios

A portfolio is a compilation of material, sometimes an assembly of artworks or other creative material, or a collection of documents and other work products. The materials in the latter type of portfolio are usually linked together by pieces of reflective writing and will often illustrate the development of knowledge, skills and abilities over a period of time. There may be an introductory synthesis paper that pulls together all of the evidence into a coherent whole.

Portfolios are a popular form of assessment, especially in professional, post-experience and art-based courses. The UK's Chartered Institute of Library and Information Professionals' (CILIP) Framework of Qualifications is portfolio-based and many teaching in higher or further education courses use a portfolio as the principal means of assessment. You may therefore have had to create one yourself but not thought to use this as an approach when designing your own teaching and learning activities.

Portfolios will only be appropriate for a long-term relationship with learners, as a portfolio cannot be created easily over only a couple of weeks. However, if you do run a longer module or course on information literacy, portfolios could be an excellent way of showing the development of learning and reflection.

You may want to encourage evidence of searches or an understanding of information as a component in a portfolio covering wider issues – for example, the now common Personal Development Plan (PDP) in UK higher education.

When designing assessments that use portfolios, think about:

- Requiring evidence that shows a progression or that allows for reflection. Something like an ongoing search for information on a subject can allow the learner to show changes in search strategy, the following of trails and the translation of a reference or abstract into the thing itself, and its subsequent use to create a new piece of work.
- Providing examples of evidence and reflective writing. Although this is becoming more common, it can still be difficult for those unused to reflective writing to produce a portfolio. This can be especially true when

working with young adults as reflective approaches are not widely used in schools, and it can be difficult to find models of good portfolios.

- Making sure that evidence exists to illustrate the portfolio – handouts, diagrams, etc.
- Ensure that sufficient guidance is provided on how to structure the portfolio.
- Drawing up clear assessment criteria.

✓ BEST FOR

- educational or staff development settings
- whole courses.

✚ MORE

- There are many online portfolio tools available (such as PebblePad, www.pebblepad.co.uk), which can work very effectively within structured course environments.
- A blog can be used to build a portfolio – they are chronological and so can develop over time. They can also be enhanced by images and other media. Most blogs enable you to keep the blog private, but having a public blog can encourage comments from peers that may help reflection and provide formative feedback.
- Remember that a portfolio can embrace a range of media – your learners might want to submit moving images, pictures and sound recordings as well as more traditional text-based content. This can be a good way of encouraging creativity.
- Use a portfolio approach to reflect on your own teaching – compile evidence and reflect on it over the course of a year.

❖ WATCH OUT

- Very high levels of motivation are needed to compile a portfolio – this is an ongoing process so you will need to provide a rationale that convinces learners to engage, as well as provide a lot of support for the process. It is probably the most time-intensive form of assessment for learners to complete, so do not approach this lightly.

82 Poster tours

Poster tours are a very effective but under-used approach to collaborative creation of content and peer assessment. They are a relatively easy way to energize a session, provide opportunities for learners to share experience and peer-assess each other's work.

You will need a flip chart and pens and somewhere to put the flip-chart paper around the room.

Divide your group into smaller groups – probably four or five groups will work best. Write a problem or issue for discussion on the same number of flip-chart sheets as there are groups. Ask each group to stand by one of the sheets and then ask them to discuss the problem or issue. For example, each group could discuss the merits of a different database, list keywords for particular search problems or produce a research strategy for different types of assessments (for a presentation, essay, etc.). Groups should write down their comments on the sheets. After a few minutes (no more than five minutes, or gauge when input is flagging), walk around yourself and ask the groups to move on to the next sheet in a clockwise direction. They should then take up the new topic, commenting on the previous group's work and adding new things themselves. This carries on until they return to their initial sheet. Be prepared at this point for some lively discussion as they see what comments have been made on their initial thoughts.

✓ BEST FOR

- collaborative creation of content and peer assessment
- group teaching
- staff development contexts
- stimulating debate
- encouraging participation.

✚ MORE

- Try using music to energize the activity – it can work with some groups but be careful on the choice of music, as you do not want it to become a version of musical chairs.
- Join the groups as they walk around, adding your own comments and prompting input if it is unforthcoming.
- Instead of writing issues on the sheets yourself, ask learners to produce something in their groups and then share it with the wider group, using a poster tour rather than presenting their work. For example, ask the groups to find information on a topic and describe their search strategy on sheets, represent the view of a question from the perspective of a particular stakeholder or ask them to produce an outline of a teaching session. Groups are asked to critique the work as they go around the sheets, providing some peer assessment. This is an effective way of engaging learners in peer assessment and usually works better than asking for comments on a group's presentation.
- A poster tour is essentially a primitive wiki – you could run the same exercise using that online tool.

❗ WATCH OUT

- Poster tours need some physical space. They do not always work very well in a cramped room as participants cannot see the posters and it can be hard to hear discussions in an enthusiastic hubbub.
- People are often unwilling to comment on other learners' work so be prepared to prompt and encourage contirbutions. Once they have made the first comment they will usually be fine.

83 Presentations by learners

Presentations by learners can be a very effective form of assessment for a variety of reasons. First of all, the format and requirements are usually easily understood by learners, so less tutor input is required to explain what learners need to do. Secondly, presentations are often straightforward to assess, either by peer, tutor, self, external lecturers or any combination of those groups. Finally, presentations may not require a lot of additional technology or equipment so can be set up and delivered with little fuss or minimal administrative work.

So, pragmatically, presentations can be easy to arrange and use. More importantly, pedagogically they can be very effective in assessing whether a range of learning outcomes have been met, including content knowledge and transferable skills. Presentations can be used flexibly, set as the final product of a task (group or individual) or at an interim point (for example, reporting on progress so far before a final report, portfolio, etc.)

When asking learners to present the results of their work you should:

- Allow sufficient time: factor in time taken to set up their presentation (even if this is to tack up a sheet of flip-chart paper or put a memory stick into a computer). Also allow some time for questions – from you and/or their peers in the audience.
- If the idea of using a presentation has been introduced within your session, give the learners the time to elect a spokesperson or to plan what they are going to say. Also provide enough warning about deadlines – give your learners both a ten- and a five-minute warning. There will be some groups in any session that have not written anything until prompted.
- Give clear instructions on what you expect from the presentation – how detailed it should be, what format, etc.
- Always respond to the presentations and give praise when it is due. Try to have a question ready to ask of each presentation.
- If the presentation is the result of several weeks' work and not simply at the end of a single workshop, then offer some input on good presentation skills.

- Be aware of the learners' nerves and take this into account when providing feedback.

✓ BEST FOR

- group work
- staff development.

✚ MORE

- Presentations are most often used in face-to-face teaching and learning situations, but they can be also made available through a VLE or other online service. Learners could be asked to prepare a presentation, perhaps with an accompanying audio recording to upload to the VLE and then assessment takes place over a period of time. This approach also means that good presentations can be made more widely available, either as a shared learning resource or as the equivalent of a showreel, demonstrating the high quality of the work produced by your learners. This option may be very helpful if you are involved in developing employability skills amongst your learners in addition to their information literacy.
- Think about whether it might be interesting to use more tightly defined presentation formats like PechaKucha (www.pecha-kucha.org), Lightning Talks (www.perl.com/pub/2004/07/30/lightningtalk.html) or Ignite (http://ignite.oreilly.com/faq/how-to.html). All these formats are time-constrained and usually specify how many slides or what technology may be used. PechaKucha is a format originally used in the creative industries. It was initially devised as an evening entertainment and networking format (the first PechaKucha Night was held in Tokyo in 2003). Originally it consisted of around a dozen presentations, with each presenter having 20 slides, each shown for 20 seconds. So each presenter had 6 minutes 40 seconds to explain his or her ideas before the next presenter took the stage. Conceived as a networking approach through which young designers could meet, show their work, exchange ideas, the format means that presentations need to be concise and fast-paced. Presenters must grant PechaKucha Night certain non-exclusive rights and license to reproduce their appearance. Variations of PechaKucha have started to appear at conferences worldwide.

84 Problem-based learning (PBL)

Problem-based learning (PBL) is a student-centred pedagogic approach in which learners work collaboratively to solve problems and reflect on their experiences. It was pioneered and used extensively at McMaster University in Canada. It has also been widely applied in the UK within medical education.

PBL draws on social-cultural and constructivist theories of learning. Instead of presenting learners with information and asking them to understand and memorize it, PBL means the learners find out for themselves. Learners often find this approach more interesting and interactive and there is evidence that it leads to deeper learning, allowing learners to construct their own understanding.

Key characteristics of PBL include:

- The teacher is a facilitator, rather than the focus of learning. His or her role is to help the learners devise effective questions and strategies to resolve the problem.
- The problems may be messy, real-life issues. The focus is on providing challenging and open-ended problems.
- There is a strong focus on collaborative working, with learners being encouraged to take responsibility for their group and for setting and meeting their learning outcomes.

Advocates of PBL argue that it is a more realistic and authentic approach to learning in real life, by virtue of being open-ended, collaborative and outcome-focused. Learners are encouraged to research, discuss and explore issues during the PBL process, using a variety of learning strategies and approaches.

If you are thinking about delivering a presentation or giving a handout – i.e. transmitting information to learners – think about how you can revise it so that the learners find this information out for themselves. What questions could you ask so that the learners can find out for themselves? Can these questions be incorporated into a scenario? For example, ask the learners to explore a database and then write a short user guide to it. This will almost certainly lead to a greater understanding of the resource than simply asking them to use it.

✓ BEST FOR

- making learning interactive, relevant and interesting
- group learning
- learning by doing.

+ MORE

- Enquiry-based learning (EBL, 'inquiry' or IBL in American English) is a related activity, which can be seen to encompass PBL but also a broader range of activities. EBL differs in that learners can define the problem themselves. EBL can be individual whereas PBL is usually a group activity; EBL may focus on research questions rather than problems. Both approaches are, however, learner-centred. Kahn and O'Rourke (2004) include small-scale investigations, such as case studies and fieldwork, along with research projects and PBL, under the umbrella of EBL.
- WebQuests (http://webquest.org/index.php) could be used for both PBL and EBL. (See **WebQuests**.)

: WATCH OUT

- PBL can take a while to set up but it can be very powerful and effective.
- Make sure that the problems are challenging. There may well be some resistance from learners who expect to be given answers (this is especially true in some educational traditions). Giving clear instructions and guidelines on what is expected and why, is very important for successful PBL.
- You also need to ensure that support systems and structures are working effectively. Given a research problem, ensure that your learners will not rush to the enquiry desk asking for the answer to their query.
- Learners at some levels will require more guidance than others and you will need to take this into account when designing your PBL. Provide a scaffolded approach where learners are guided through the problem-

solving process (for example, use a technique like a WebQuest).

➥ REFERENCES

Kahn, P. and O'Rourke, K. (2004) *Guide to Curriculum Design: enquiry-based learning,* Higher Education Academy, www.heacademy.ac.uk/resources/ detail/resource_database/id359_guide_to_curriculum_design_ebl.

85 Pub quizzes

This is based on the type of quiz commonly held in UK pubs, which uses common question formats for different rounds of the quiz. This is a useful way to inject some competition into a group session. It is particularly good at making a dry subject like referencing more interesting.

Break a larger group into teams – let the groups self-select their teams or choose them yourself. Try and arrange each team at a separate table. Ask each team to come up with a suitable team name and explain that you will be asking them questions in a series of rounds. You could include the notion of a joker round, counting double. Provide answer sheets and ask teams to swap answer sheets for marking at the end of each round. Use sweets or similar incentives for the winners of each round and/or the overall contest.

Run through the quiz – typical pub quiz rounds include identifying pictures or sounds, so see if you can work these in. For example, for a referencing pub quiz you could have rounds on referencing books, journals, websites, etc. The picture round could be a simple missing word on the screen or the referencing of a picture. The sound (music) round could be to fill in the missing words on a sound file – give your quiz invention free reign.

✓ BEST FOR

- large groups
- referencing or other dry topics.

+ MORE

- Try running this within a VLE or online – teams could play against one another in real time or play the machine by using time-released answers.

⁇ WATCH OUT

- Be sure to get your timing right with the rounds – allow discussion and marking time as well as time for deciding on the team names. This nearly always takes longer than you expect.

- Pub quizzes are common in the UK but might not be understood in some cultures. Call it whatever you want, as the concept is not exclusive to a pub environment!

86 Questionnaires

Questionnaires can be used in several different ways in your planning and evaluation. One way is as part of the audit process. You might wish to distribute a questionnaire to learners before you meet them to audit what they already know, gauge their interest and check their skill levels. They are also used to obtain feedback on programmes or sessions.

When designing a questionnaire:

- Think about whether you want qualitative (descriptive) or quantitative (measurable) data – or indeed both. If quantitative, remember that there are dangers in a five-point scale. Learners might tend to neutrality – saying that it was OK – not great and not bad. Denying them the middle point in the scale seems mean, but at least you get a more decisive result.
- When using a quantitative scale for questions, ensure there is a balance of options – for example a scale of 'Outstanding, Excellent, Very Good, Poor' doesn't provide an option between Very Good and Poor.
- Qualitative data requires a box to complete. Online this can be expandable but on paper you are forced to have a finite space. Think carefully about whether you are asking too many questions or leaving too much blank space: both can intimidate!
- Only ask questions to which you want an answer. Few people enjoy filling questionnaires in and it is even more tedious analysing them (unless you have an optical mark reader or it can be done online). A few well targeted questions are better than a number of vaguely relevant ones.
- Ask learners to comment on the score they have given if you do use a quantitative scale. Receiving a poor score is useless – you will want to know what was wrong so that you can rectify it.
- Make the text attractive to read – ensure you use a good clear font and provide instructions on how to complete the form.
- If you have asked for self-assessment, e.g. 'on a scale how experienced are you in —' then try to find a way to check the score through

subsidiary questions. Learners will often inflate or underestimate their experience and knowledge based on a perception of what the teacher wants or on what it might mean for the subsequent session if they answer in a particular way.

- Always give a rationale as to why you want the learners to complete the questionnaire. This can be done on the questionnaire or in person. Give them time to do it and thank them afterwards.
- Ensure your questionnaire links back to the aims and learning outcomes of the session – ask questions to gather opinion on whether learners feel these have been met.

✓ BEST FOR

- auditing groups online
- short, targeted feedback – a few questions at the end of a session.

✚ MORE

- Instead of a whole group approach, try sampling. The results will probably be very similar and you will not be faced with a large pile to analyse.
- Use an online survey and send a link to learners after the event – you may find this more successful than chasing learners to fill a form in at the end of an event when they are trying to leave.

✱ WATCH OUT

- Try to find out if your learners are being bombarded with questionnaires. If so, then they are unlikely to welcome another one and you should find another method. Perhaps include an incentive, such as a prize draw, for respondents to the questionnaire.

87 Quizzes

Quizzes and tests are a very popular way of assessing learning – they are relatively quick to design, are understood by most learners and can be quickly checked. However, they are also often trite, pitched at the wrong level and pointless in the learners' eyes. Make sure that:

- the questions are related to the learning that has gone on before
- the questions are relevant to the learners' interests and needs – they need to see a point to the exercise
- they are not too hard (which will lead to frustration) or too easy (boredom)
- they are not impossible to complete by an average learner in the time allocated
- the tasks asked by the quiz are easy to understand
- answers are given out.

Most learners will be willing to take a quiz or test if they see it is related to the teaching that has taken place and they can see a return for their time (it will reinforce and consolidate their learning).

Quizzes and tests are probably best kept short and easy to understand – hence the success of multiple-choice exercises – but, like all assessment, they should be linked directly to the learning outcomes.

✓ BEST FOR

- younger learners
- online assessments
- quick assessments.

✚ MORE

- Try running the quiz as a competitive exercise – break the quiz into rounds (see **Pub quizzes**) or give small prizes for the quickest correct answers. Matching the format of the latest popular TV quiz is often a good idea but can take some time to set up.

- Use images to make a test more appealing.
- Vary the simple question–answer format by asking learners to fill in blanks or click and drag if online.
- Try to keep quizzes to one side of A4 or one screen. If you need to have a longer test then either split it up across the session, or look at another way of checking whether your learning outcomes have been achieved.
- Online quizzes are simple to create. For example, Quia Web (www.quia.com/web) is a low-cost quiz site that will also host your quiz. You may also have access to a VLE that contains quiz tools. Bear in mind that although an online quiz is technically simple to create, it still requires the use of good, relevant questions.
- If this is a quiz you will use regularly, make a note of common issues that learners have trouble with or get wrong – this will enable you to be prepared for those issues next time. You may choose to adapt your teaching to ensure learners are better prepared for the test, or alternatively the test can act as formative assessment and provide a memorable way of learning (that is, learning from mistakes).

⁙ WATCH OUT

- Quizzes can often be a lazy form of assessment. They can be easy to cheat on and need to be carefully contextualized if they are not to be seen as a chore by learners.
- Tests can remind learners of unpleasant failures in the past. If it is to be marked in some way then you should signal this to the learners at the start. If it is not to be marked then there needs to be a clear rationale presented for the test – why should they try something that has no measurable outcome?
- If the test or quiz is to be diagnostic then you will need to collect it quickly and have some way of marking it in time to amend your planning. If this is actually in the session you will benefit from it being part of team teaching. Your partner can engage the learners whilst you check the tests.

88 Self-assessment

Self-assessment can be a useful part of your assessment strategy. It allows learners to find out whether the learning outcomes of the session or course have been met, without having to submit their work for assessment by other people. It may seem as if the teacher is transferring responsibility for the assessment, so it does require a clear and supportive framework in order to work:

- Publish the assessment criteria and explain it to the learners. They will need to know what they are looking for in their own learning.
- Provide checklists for learners to work through when assessing their own work.
- If you use workbooks, be sure to include answer sheets.

A sample self-assessment exercise might be based around finding and evaluating information. Ask the learners to find a journal on a topic. Set clear criteria for the type of article that you want it to be – perhaps published after a particular date, of academic content or from a newspaper. Once they have found an article, ask the learners to reference it correctly and write a short abstract. Allot marks for each element and then ask the learners to mark against the criteria. You could take on the role of second marker to check how well it has worked.

✓ BEST FOR

- assessing simple and practical learning outcomes
- staff development
- learners with a short-term engagement with your teaching
- encouraging learners to take 'ownership' of their learning.

✚ MORE

- Develop online exercises with built-in feedback. This can be attached to each question of a simple multiple-choice exercise. For example: 'You answered A. The correct answer was B', or in more detail: 'You answered A and the answer is B because —.' Most assessment software allows you to do this automatically.

❣ WATCH OUT

- Self-assessment needs trust between learner and teacher – it demands that learners take responsibility for their own learning – and can be scary when you first try it.

89 Self-guided tours

The tour has long been a staple of any induction process. When groups are small, the personal tour given by a knowledgeable guide to buildings and services can still be the most effective method. However, where time is short or where groups are too big, a self-guided tour is a reasonable alternative. This requires good planning and co-ordination. The best self-guided tours are flexible enough for learners to choose their own routes. Self-guided tours can be via written guides or maps, using static displays at points around a building, in the form of audio guides, entirely delivered online using graphics, pictures or film, or a combination of all of the above. However they are delivered, they should:

- Allow for multiple start and finish points. If a learner has not completed the tour in one go they should be able to rejoin later without having to start from scratch.
- Keep any information to short, focused inputs. The power of the more conversational personal tours is in the anecdotes and contextualization that the tour guide can include – self-guided tours can still do this but it is harder to gauge reaction so keep them to a minimum.
- If you are using technology then ensure that the technical standards are high. You will be compared with examples from outside your organization (such as museums). If you do not have access to a media department or internal expertise, plus time to work on the technology, then think carefully about proceeding. Amateur videos may look endearing for a minute but their charms will fade very quickly.
- Take the tour yourself – how long does it take, are the instructions clear, does it cover all of things that you actually see?
- Introduce the rationale for the tour and include how long it will take in the introduction. Learners can often see it as being second best compared with a personal tour so a clear rationale is important to convincing them to invest their time.
- Be careful in using old tours – things can change very quickly and your format should be flexible enough to allow speedy inserts.

✓ BEST FOR

- large groups.

✚ MORE

- Have a mixed economy approach. For example, you might meet and greet the group and have a demonstration/hands-on activity with the catalogue and then send them off with a self-guided tour of the building. Where possible, include the chance for the group to ask questions as what they want to know may not match exactly what you want to tell them.

❗ WATCH OUT

- Induction is primarily about setting an atmosphere. Very little information will stick at this stage so don't overload. Try to include some interaction with (friendly and welcoming) staff as part of the self-guided process so that learners will want to return.

90 Social bookmarking

Social bookmarking sites enable users to record their favourite websites and any other pages they wish to keep as a reference. The references are stored on the social bookmarking site and can be accessed by the user, unlike browser bookmarks (or favourites), which are tied to a computer. As well as storing and organizing the bookmarks for the user's own reference, they can also be shared – hence the 'social' aspect. There are many social bookmarking sites, such as delicious (www.delicious.com), Digg (http://digg.com) and Diigo (www.diigo.com).

There are several ways that these sites can be used to enhance information skills teaching. One simple example is to store a list of references within the social bookmarking site and make this public to your learners. Most sites allow you to annotate the resources, so you can explain why the sites are useful. This can be used as an additional resource for your teaching, but also used within hands-on sessions. If your learners have an account for the site you are using, they will be able to add their own comments on the resources.

✓ BEST FOR

- creating resource lists for use within teaching sessions or as an additional reference
- sharing resources between learners.

+ MORE

- Teach your learners about RSS feeds and how they can subscribe. For example, use a tool such as iGoogle (www.google.com/ig). As part of this session, get your learners to subscribe to your social bookmarks using the in-built RSS feeds. They will then be automatically alerted when you add new resources.
- Set a task, either individual or group, where learners have to create their own resource list, justifying the choice of resources using the comments

feature. These resources can then be shared with peers.

- Lists of social bookmarks can be exported in different formats, which can be useful as a reference. Diigo, for example, has the facility to export to Internet Explorer, CSV (which can be read in Excel) and delicious – this means a delicious user can upload the bookmarks to their own account.
- Consider using a more academic social bookmarking site, such as Connotea (www.connotea.org), CiteULike (www.citeulike.org) or Mendeley (www.mendeley.com).
- Explore the differences in functionality and usability between social bookmarking software and commercial reference management packages.

❢ WATCH OUT

- Don't feel you have to start from scratch creating bookmark lists – most social bookmarking sites have the ability to import bookmarks or favourites from your web browser.
- Depending on how you use social bookmarking sites, your learners may need training on how to use the site and will need to have an account. As these sites provide a useful way of saving and managing web resources, you may wish to make this the focus of one of your sessions.

91 Stop, Start, Continue feedback

This method comes from Phil Race and is an excellent way to get quick, qualitative feedback from a group.

Give each learner three sticky notes at the start of the session. On each note ask them to write STOP, START and CONTINUE. Explain that the purpose of the exercise is to gather their thoughts on the session and that they should write on the notes anything that they want you to stop doing (because it is not working or that they already know perhaps), something that they want you to start doing (what they expected you to cover and you have not) and something that they want you to continue (it is really useful or well done). They should do this as the session progresses rather than leaving it to the end. The sticky notes are clearly anonymous and they should not feel pressured to write something on each one.

At a point in the session when you want feedback (typically, but not always, a coffee break or at the end of the session), ask the learners to stick the notes on the door (or wall, board, etc.) as they leave. You might wish to vary this by asking them to stick the notes up at a break in the session – this way gives you the option to change something for the rest of the session.

When analysing the notes take care not to concentrate on the 'stop' sections – these are important but remember the validation offered by the 'continue' notes too.

✓ BEST FOR

- quick feedback
- constructive feedback. A simple feedback form often elicits no more than generally positive affirmations of good practice. This approach often gets more effective developmental responses.

✚ MORE

- If sticky notes are not available you could simply give the learners a single sheet with three boxes labelled STOP, START and CONTINUE. This is perhaps a little less 'odd' and therefore less threatening for the learners.

❣ WATCH OUT

- Sticky notes have a strange attraction for some people and you may find that they prefer to take them away rather than use them for feedback. The single-sheet option above is better if this is the case.
- You will get silly or unsettling remarks at some point in your teaching career. Try not to be too downhearted or upset by them. Telling you that you should 'stop wearing that tie/dress' is almost certainly intended to be 'clever' rather than destructive – ignore it and go for the ones that can advance the learning (unless the tie/dress truly is awful!).

➥ REFERENCES

Race, P. (ed.) (1999) 2000 Tips for Lecturers, Kogan Page.

92 Storytelling

Once upon a time...

Storytelling can be both a metaphor for the learning and teaching event and a pedagogic practice.

First of all, when considering the former, storytelling presupposes a beginning, middle and end, with a narrative connection between each part and some form of conclusion. This can be a helpful way of structuring a class. It suggests the importance of the introduction in setting the scene, expectations and establishing the style. You might wish to think of ways of drawing in participants. The middle needs to have a clear logical progression with each stage linked together. The conclusion draws all the different elements together, with the expectation that something has been completed. As a metaphor, a learning and teaching event can be considered as a story or a journey, with narrative explanation.

But storytelling can also serve a more fundamental purpose in the very practice of teaching. There is some discussion of storytelling or 'narrative pedagogy' in the literature. Some of the key strands are:

- development of a narrative
- establishment of personal interest
- use of character
- recognition of emotions and feelings
- some form of change/event
- episodes for reflection and learning.

You may also use storytelling for case study accounts.

Stories are important in setting a context for the learning. Learners will process information more easily if they can place it into a familiar context – this has been at the heart of fairy-tales and storytelling for centuries. Personal experience can provide powerful reinforcement of key concepts and also reassure that mistakes and problems are normal in the information seeking process. Think of times when you or your colleagues have experienced difficulties or successes in finding and using information. Think of contexts that fit your learners' experiences and contexts and weave a narrative that incorporates them. This does not need to be complicated – it can simply be setting an example or case study for nurses in a hospital setting.

The story simply provides the framework in which the learning takes place.

✓ BEST FOR

- Most groups will respond to a story if it is well told.

✚ MORE

- Incorporate your stories into gaming. This is especially effective in online contexts where the material is often very dry. Most learners are now familiar with online games even if they are not active gamers themselves. They will expect a narrative – it could be a learner approaching an information forest or an identifiable individual collecting the elements needed to solve an information puzzle.
- Storytelling can also be used as a method of assessment. Ask learners to create a story rather than writing an essay or a straightforward presentation. This is a more creative method of assessment that may be more engaging and reflective, although learners may need some guidance in the approach to take with their story.
- Digital storytelling offers the benefits of using technology to enhance the story and engage learners. Using multimedia, such as images and music, will demonstrate a range of information literacies as learners will need to understand how different media can be used to convey different moods and concepts. Easy to use tools such as Animoto (http://animoto.com) and VoiceThread (http://voicethread.com) can be used to create a digital story.

❢ WATCH OUT

- You will need to match the story to the learners. It can be easy to bore or patronize if you get the level and context wrong. Try out your storytelling with short tales. Long stories will amuse and possibly engage, but the essential point you wish to make may be lost.

93 Technology-enhanced learning (TEL)

Technology-enhanced learning (TEL) is the practice of using technology to extend the scope of your teaching. It should be an essential part of your teaching repertoire. TEL may be based within a VLE like Moodle or Blackboard, using the functions provided, or it may utilize a range of different technologies and platforms. TEL is a development from older terms such as online learning, e-learning or computer-assisted learning.

TEL has evident advantages in creating interactive and engaging learning and teaching environments for distance learners. It can be used in all kinds of learning and teaching opportunities, complementing and extending face-to-face delivery by providing access to more material, enabling interactivity and creating collaborative virtual spaces. Good TEL broadens the scope of your work, and can be used in classroom environments as well as the more customary remote, asynchronous learning events.

Allow plenty of time to design and plan your learning materials. It will be just as time-consuming and labour-intensive as preparing for face-to-face teaching and should be approached with the same underlying principles in mind: auditing your learners, having flexible plans with clear aims and learning outcomes, delivering interesting and innovative teaching inputs and activities, designing appropriate assessments and gathering feedback to enhance reflection. What will be different from face-to-face teaching are the ways that you will design your teaching/information inputs and the range of opportunities available for assessment and interaction.

Salmon (2004, 26) describes a five-stage model of teaching and learning online. This is a very helpful starting point when planning TEL as it suggests what you need to do to get it to work properly. The stages are:

1 Access and motivation through welcoming and encouraging participants, ensuring everyone can log on, etc.
2 Online socialization by creating a learning community, getting participants to send and receive messages.
3 Information exchange through facilitating tasks and supporting the use of

learning materials.

4   Knowledge construction through discussion and debate and the completion of individual and group activities.

5   Development by providing links outside the immediate learning environment and supporting independent learning.

Try using this five-stage model to assess how effectively you have planned your TEL.

✓ BEST FOR

- distance learners
- learners who have easy access to technology
- computer labs.

✚ MORE

- If you are writing a tutorial, tell your learners how long each online activity will take to complete.
- Make individual activities short and quick. Each segment of online text or activity should fit onto a screen rather than being so long to read or complex to understand that the learner will need to scroll down the page or read the instructions more than once.
- Make your learning materials interactive – most people want to do something with the mouse when reading from a screen and the longer you delay this then the more likely they are to lose interest, and at worst, log off.
- Make the TEL relevant: generic examples may mean you can reuse your carefully crafted content very easily but learners are more likely to engage if you can match activities to their real needs. This is often achieved by allowing your learners to enter their examples (into a search engine, for example) and then asking for an analysis of the results or by asking them to create resources.
- Always give feedback on assessments – computer-generated responses to answers replicate the formative feedback that you would give in a face-to-face session.
- Learners will almost certainly type something into a search box as soon as they see it. If you want them to read something first then it may be wise to put it on a different page.

- Think about accessibility – there are many guides and checks for you to test your pages against relevant standards, such as the WAVE tool (http://wave. webaim.org).
- Remember usability as well as accessibility. Usability means making the pages as easy and intuitive to use as possible – beware of over-designing your pages. If what you are thinking of doing doesn't advance the learning, don't do it.
- Ensure that the activities used complement your face-to-face teaching and that both meet your aims and outcomes. Often you may expect too little or too much of your learners in an online environment – remember your learners are still the same no matter which medium is used. For example, a simple quiz is still a simple quiz even if it is online and enhanced with images and other effects.
- Try to build in a 'hook' that engages the learners. Dropout rates for online learning are much higher than for face-to-face working and something that makes the learner care can be very effective in combating this.

....

Case study *Liberation at the University of Northampton*
....

The original Liberation concept was for a suite of short, interactive, relevant and personalized online tutorials (Powis and Payne, 2001). The intention was to provide alternatives to face-to-face tutorials and as the library team found that it was being asked to deliver increasing numbers of sessions on referencing, a Harvard tutorial was a natural fit for the Liberation suite.

The team felt that teaching referencing was notoriously dull so they wanted a hook, something to amuse without patronizing. The development team hit on the idea of rewarding or punishing a cartoon cat and Harvey sprang from that. One of the team was artistic so drew Harvey, and the web developer built the tutorial around his adventures. The actual exercises are short but reasonably challenging and, even if the intention amongst some students is to harm the cat, they will need to know how to reference to get it wrong enough to succeed.

The library service was committed to open access so put it on the web rather than embedded in their VLE. Evaluation was achieved via an online form on completion but a lot of positive feedback was gathered from academics who used the tutorial with their students and from universities, colleges and schools who asked to use the tutorial. Usage is high and many courses have adopted it as an, early, compulsory exercise. It has also had a long shelf life without dating as the Harvard system has not changed and Harvey does not rely on any particular cultural reference points.

Screen-shots **93.1**, **93.2**, **93.3** and **93.4** illustrate the use of Liberation.

93.1 *Introducing Harvey...*

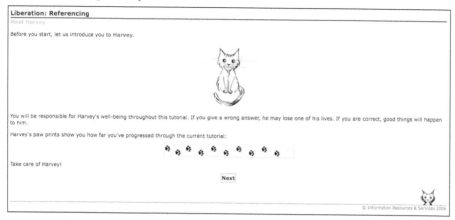

93.2 *Tutorial options*

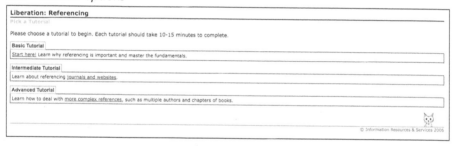

93.3 *Sample exercise (with reward) from the Basic Tutorial*

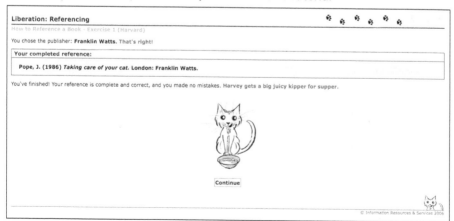

93.4 *Or if it goes wrong...*

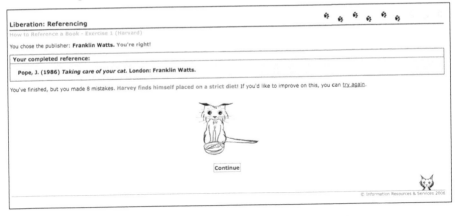

···

❖ WATCH OUT

- Make sure that your learners are ready to use the technology and that you can be assured that they have suitable levels of access. It is worth checking that you do not create a resource that will only work with a particular internet browser.
- Take the online package through as much testing as you can, preferably with colleagues who have had nothing to do with the development or with people who come from the same experience and context as the potential audience for the package. Never make assumptions without testing the material.
- TEL will require you to develop your skills, whether these are technical skills, design skills for online learning or skills such as online moderation.

❖ REFERENCES

Powis, C. and Payne G. (2001) 'Liberating' User Education: developing a web-based teaching & learning package at University College Northampton, *Vine*, **31** (1), 29–34.

Salmon, G. (2004) *E-moderating: the key to teaching and learning online*, 2nd edn, RoutledgeFalmer.

94 Treasure hunt

This is a variation on an induction activity. Set the learners a series of tasks that take them around the library, answering questions that lead them to a prize (the treasure). In doing so they should visit key areas and/or find out about services. The tasks could be a quiz/crossword, the answers to which lead up to one location containing the treasure (but be careful that these are not too dull!) or they could be in the form of actual tasks. The latter could be the construction of a map from clues or the creation of a model using materials hidden at particular locations around the building.

Make sure that you:

- Time the hunt well – you should not make it so easy that some will finish well ahead of time, or so hard that no one wins.
- Hide the treasure well – hunters should not be able to find it by accident.
- Have multiple start points that lead to the same goal – everyone starting at the same point will lead to chaos.
- Prepare answer sheets.

This activity can be surprisingly motivating for learners. A bit of competition will be both unexpected and engaging for most learners expecting a dull library session.

✓ BEST FOR

- younger learners.

✚ MORE

- The treasure could be a prize for the first completed set of correct answers rather than an object.
- Put the treasure hunt online, perhaps using Second Life (http://secondlife.com) or similar virtual environments. If you are

designing your own virtual world then you should take care that it looks and feels professional as learners expect high quality from online experiences.

❣ WATCH OUT

- Be careful about extreme competitiveness or disengagement by shy individuals if you have set up teams. Do not use the treasure hunt as an opportunity to relax – engage with the groups as they 'play' and moderate or encourage as required.
- Think about whether there will be any disruption to other parts of your service – a treasure hunt across a silent study area in revision time would be problematic!

95 Video

Videos, or any multimedia tools, are a useful way of delivering teaching remotely (the UK's Open University has been doing this for decades) and for breaking up a session – changing delivery method after 10 to 20 minutes is always a good strategy. However, some issues to consider when using video are:

- Make sure that you have the right technology. Video-streaming servers are more common now, but you may still have to use a CD or DVD and be sure that the technology in the teaching room is compatible and working. It does not reflect well if you struggle with the equipment for minutes. Always embed in your presentation or pre-load the film at the appropriate start point if possible – a seamless effect will always be better than fiddling with a machine.
- Keep the video short. Making a group watch a long film when they are expecting interaction with a teacher will frustrate and will often be seen as a poor substitute.
- If you make the film yourself then be professional. Learners are used to high-quality products – commercial TV, film, and video games. Their tolerance for amateur efforts will be low (although the culture of YouTube may be leading to more tolerance of home-made videos, this would be dangerous to assume).
- If you do not have the skills yourself, consider finding a local college where media students may be looking for project work.
- Be ruthless. If the video is no good then do not show it. Test it on a few trusted and critical learners or colleagues before you show it and take careful note of what they say. Watch the viewers when you show it – their body language will give you major clues as to its effectiveness.

✓ BEST FOR

- distance learners

- online learning
- adding variety to a session.

✚ MORE

- Try audio files or podcasts, as they are much easier to produce and edit.
- Use creating video as an activity for your learners. There are many low-cost video recorders and many mobile phones have the ability to record video. Ask your learners to record short pieces of video instead of presentations as a form of assessment (whether formal or informal).
- For instructional videos, consier creating a screencast – a video that captures the computer screen and can be used to demonstrate how to use a website or a piece of software. These can be enhanced wth an audio commentary or text onnotations. Sites like Screenr (www.screenr.com) and Jing (www.techsmith.com/jing) offer basic features for free; or consider commercial software such as Camtasia Studio (www.techsmith.com/camtasia).

❢ WATCH OUT

- If you are using a voice-over then audition people for it – voices can sound very different on an audio file. Be careful when reusing film as it (and the information it conveys) can become dated very quickly.

96 Virtual learning environments (VLEs) (or learning management systems, LMSs)

Virtual learning environments (VLEs) (or, outside the UK, learning management systems) are found most often in educational settings and can be either commercially produced or open sourced. They are online environments containing documents, exercises, assessments and teacher-controlled monitoring, assessing and management tools. They may also function as a portal for learners to access a wider array of services than their learning materials.

If the institution that you are working for or with uses a VLE then you will usually be expected to provide materials that either use its tools or fit in with it. This is actually an excellent way of integrating your material into the mainstream teaching and learning development, and will often raise your profile with both learners and teaching colleagues. As each VLE is different, it is only possible to give very general advice here:

- Get as much training on using your VLE as possible – there will usually be hidden buttons or time-saving advice that will make your job much easier.
- Use the VLE, but only if it serves a pedagogic purpose that fits your learning outcomes. Using things for the sake of them will lead to poor teaching and little learning.
- Be aware that not every user will have the same capacity in their computers. Try not to overload the VLE with too many files that require high-specification hardware or networks to run them.
- Where possible, use the tools that come with the VLE – going outside the VLE will potentially confuse learners by opening extra windows.

You may wish to develop standalone information literacy modules. It would be a good idea to check whether there are any open educational resources (OERs) you might be able to use. If you work in UK further or higher education, have a look at JORUM (www.jorum.ac.uk). Before starting on a major project, do think quite carefully whether your content will be used.

There are lots of examples of online tutorials that have taken a lot of time to create and have not been used cost-effectively.

✓ BEST FOR

- distance learners
- blended learning.

✚ MORE

- A VLE can be a straightjacket. If the VLE does not do what you want it to, and you cannot see an alternative, then go outside of it. There are many online alternatives (such as social networking sites, blogs, wikis, document sharing, etc.) that do not need web design or programming skills.

❗ WATCH OUT

- Do not use the VLE only as a document store – there are better ways to do this. Make your documents interactive or put them in for comment if you do deposit them in the VLE. Regularly check that they are still relevant and up to date and also find out the storage limits on your VLE. In commercial VLEs storage can often carry costs.

97 Visiting lecturers/guest speakers

A visiting lecturer is an external facilitator, teacher or workshop leader, usually with particular interest and experience in a specialist area. Learners can benefit from a guest speaker bringing specialist insight or knowledge to a topic. Guest speakers can also serve to vary style and/or input during a longer session. In many professional, vocational and creative subjects, experienced practitioners are used as visiting lecturers and this can apply to the teaching of information literacy.

You may wish to bring in current practitioners to talk about how they interact with information. This would work particularly well in professional subjects, like marketing or law. A group of learners hearing from a professional can be much more powerful than a librarian lecturing about what ought to be done.

You may also wish to use a data protection officer, or someone involved with information compliance to talk about data security or freedom of information. Alternatively, ask a successful learner on a course you have run to return and talk about how they approached a challenging task. This might be any kind of learner ranging from a senior school pupil talking to younger learners about reading for pleasure, to second year undergraduate talking to first years about essay research, a recent PhD student or someone who has completed family history work. Guest speakers or visiting lecturers can provide a role model or be the voice of experience to learners who may not see the relevance or application of information literacy within their research.

You should also consider the role of guest speaker or visiting lecturer for yourself. Integrating information literacy into the mainstream curriculum will significantly improve learning as students appreciate its relevance and impact on their studies. Collaboration with subject teaching staff is crucial to this but acting as a visiting lecturer, perhaps as a precursor to a more active workshop, will raise your credibility and give the idea of information literacy more gravitas.

✓ BEST FOR

- including as part of a series of sessions or to break up a long lecture.

✚ MORE

- Instead of inviting the guest lecturer to deliver their input in person they could produce a podcast or video. If you have the relevant equipment, a live link to a remote lecturer will work well, too. This can be especially effective for a question and answer session, and can work well for your input to courses that have an online element or that operate in a VLE.
- Visiting lecturers could also be involved in assessment (perhaps as a judge for presentations).

❗ WATCH OUT

- Take advice or ask around before asking anyone to deliver a lecture – recommendations from those who have seen or heard people speak can save embarrassment.
- Be careful not to ask too much of visiting lecturers – they will often be willing to do it as a favour (with expenses, naturally) but it can be easy to overuse them in your enthusiasm.

98 Voting systems

Electronic-voting systems (also called personal-response systems) are now common in education. Typically, they will consist of a number of handsets and software that will need to be loaded on to the presenter's computer. The teacher will load a series of questions into the presentation computer and display them during face-to-face teaching. Learners will use the handsets to vote for a series of options. A graphical representation of the voting is usually then displayed (and the correct answer, if appropriate). Learners can be identified or anonymous. Although questions are usually answered by TRUE or FALSE, or by choosing one of a series of options, handsets are increasingly allowing text input. This significantly increases the sophistication of the questions that can be asked although you will need to add in significantly more time per question if you ask for sentences (not everyone can text or type at speed!). Voting systems are useful for obtaining quick feedback during the session, breaking up a long session by providing interaction, checking learning by asking or testing knowledge or influencing a search strategy by choosing keywords that you subsequently use in a live search. Tips for effective use of voting systems include:

- Make the questions focused and answerable via multiple choice or, if text answers are required, answerable in a few words.
- Give the learners a few minutes to familiarize themselves with the equipment – have a quick test question to start with.
- Try not to use them if you cannot give each person a handset. If this isn't possible then give time for consultation before asking for a group response.

✓ BEST FOR

- breaking up sessions that would otherwise be dominated by the teacher
- quick feedback
- quick formative assessments.

✚ MORE

- If you do not have access to the handset system you can still use voting by utilizing coloured cards – answer = red, green or blue, etc. This can be just as energizing for a group and is a lot less likely to go wrong!
- There are also voting websites where users can vote via text message, such as SMS Poll (www.smspoll.net) or Polleverywhere (www.polleverywhere.com).

❗ WATCH OUT

- Be careful not to overuse voting systems, as they can quickly become a gimmick. This is especially true if they are heavily used elsewhere in your institution.

99 WebQuests

A WebQuest is a structured web-based activity. It is defined on the WebQuest home page as 'an inquiry-oriented lesson format in which most or all of the information the learners work with comes from the web' (http://webquest.org.). Bernie Dodge at San Diego State University developed WebQuests in 1995. There are tools available to create WebQuests, but the simple structure can be created on any web page or using a program such as Word or PowerPoint which can contain web links. They are ideal for use in information skills teaching as they focus on finding and using information, aiming to foster higher-order thinking, based around problem solving, analysis and synthesis.

WebQuests have a standard structure that is used as a framework for guiding the learner. Depending on the level of the learner and your learning outcomes, you can give as much or as little guidance to the learner as you desire. WebQuests can be used for a variety of purposes (see http://webquest.sdsu.edu/taskonomy.html). This page provides a useful guide to different types of WebQuest and explains how information is used in each task. For example, is it simple information reproduction or is synthesis or judgement involved?

The structure normally involves an Introduction, Task, Process, Resources, Evaluation and Conclusion:

- Introduction: an overview of what is expected in the WebQuest.
- Task: a specific question or problem for your learners to address.
- Process: guidance on how learners should approach the task. This contains as much or as little information as you feel is appropriate for your learners.
- Resources: a selection of resources to be used in the WebQuest. These are normally web resources, but can be paper based. You may guide your learners directly to the resources they need to use, or perhaps to a directory site where the learners have to locate a resource for themselves. This can then test search and evaluation skills.

- Evaluation: what is required in terms of output from the WebQuest, which may include marking criteria. The output could be a report, presentation or something more creative.
- Conclusion: a summary which may include encouraging reflection on the task.

Examples may be found in Further Reading (below).

✓ BEST FOR

- providing a structure for your learning tasks
- encouraging higher level thinking
- guided tasks involving web resources.

✛ MORE

- Despite the name, a WebQuest doesn't have to be on the web! The simple structure could be used in a printed handout, pointing to resources contained in a library or elsewhere.
- Consider using an authoring tool to create your WebQuest – a list of tools can be found at: www.webquest.org/index-create.php.

❣ WATCH OUT

- Attention spans can be much shorter while learning online so make sure that there is plenty of interaction and an interesting 'story' to keep learners engaged.

→ FURTHER READING

Information literacy and research webquest,
https://sites.google.com/a/parkrose.k12.or.us/information-literacy-webquest/home.
Jurassic Park – an information literacy webquest,
http://fayette.k12.in.us/~cbeard/jp/webquest.html.

100 Wikis

Wikis are online collaborative tools that are relatively easy to set up (they often come as part of a VLE) and can be useful in both the preparation of your teaching and as a teaching tool.

Wikis work by allowing you to type documents that can then be searched for and edited by others – Wikipedia is an obvious example of a dynamic and evolving wiki. The key to using them is to be accepting that your finely crafted prose may be edited in a way that you do not necessarily like – the resultant document will be an example of the 'wisdom of crowds'. This can be liberating but it can also be distressing at first.

Wikis can be used in teaching to aid planning or preparation. Put your plans or ideas into a wiki and ask colleagues to add comments or make changes. You may be able to use them to audit your users if they have access to a wiki before your session. Post a topic and ask for your learners to describe what they want and need to know on it – this might be different for individuals but you should see the learners come to some sort of consensus.

✓ BEST FOR

- continuing assessment
- instant feedback.

+ MORE

As a teaching tool, wikis can be used by learners – a whole group or smaller groups as you can set up distinct editing privileges for particular pages – to construct their work. Examples include:

- Giving learners a series of topics to research and then see their entries grow organically as they research and add to the wiki page.
- Set up a wiki for learners to build up a set of tips for and/or evaluation of databases or resources.
- Make a wiki available throughout your session for learners to add key things that they have learned as the session goes on.

! WATCH OUT

- Learners will often be reluctant to add to something if they think that it might be changed. They can also be reluctant to be the first to post something, so seeding your wiki with initial comments is often a good idea. Wikis can be disorienting as learners see their input disappear, so prepare them for this. Most will have used Wikipedia but very few will have added anything in this sort of environment so a good induction is essential.
- You need to set parameters for access as wikis are easy to abuse.
- Do not use wikis as a gimmick – as with all electronic systems they can be used simply because they are there. There should always be a good educational reason for using them.

101 Worksheets

Worksheets or workbooks are a popular way to assess information skills. Typically given out to complete during the hands-on section of a workshop, worksheets can be a useful framework for learners to work through a series of exercises that practice and reinforce the skills taught in the workshop. They are generally easy to put together – just create a question based on each point made during the workshop. However, worksheets can be very mechanistic and are often pitched at the lowest common denominator, which can make them very easy and unchallenging for the learner.

When writing them:

- Do not write a series of questions – this is a quiz and not a worksheet.
- Write short pieces around each of the questions, which puts them into context.
- Provide answer sheets.

✓ BEST FOR

- hands-on workshops
- reinforcing learning at a distance or after a session
- providing scaffolds for learning.

✚ MORE

- Instead of simple question and answer sheets, have missing words or phrases (drag and click, if online) or flow charts that lack key elements. The key is having a contextual base for the exercise and, like all forms of assessment, making it relevant and worth the time of both learner and teacher.
- A worksheet can also take the form of a writing frame – a handout given to learners in order to guide the creation of a required piece of work, such as an essay. A writing frame provides prompts and gives a suggested structure for the learner's work. Depending on the amount of help you wish to provide the learner, the writing frame can be detailed or

simple. A writing frame is an example of scaffolded learning where you do not expect the learner to do everything for themselves – you provide a scaffold which the learner can use to build on. You may also hear writing frames referred to as 'writing scaffolds'.

❗ WATCH OUT

- Worksheets are easy to produce and often easy to complete. Learners need to be challenged for real learning to take place so be careful to make sure that your worksheets are valued by the learners – do they represent a value for the time given up by the learner to complete them?

Index